WITHDRAWN

AMERICAN REVOLUTIONARY

Alexander McDougall.
PORTRAIT FOR McDOUGALL DESCENDANTS BY JAMES PATTON, FROM MINIATURE BY RAMAGE, NEW-YORK HISTORICAL SOCIETY, COURTESY MR. AND MRS. JOHN L. HAWKES.

AMERICAN REVOLUTIONARY

A Biography of General Alexander McDougall

William L. MacDougall
Foreword by Richard B. Morris

Contributions in American History, Number 57

GREENWOOD PRESS
Westport, Connecticut • London, England

Library of Congress Cataloging in Publication Data

MacDougall, William L
   American revolutionary.

   (Contributions in American history ; no. 57)
   Bibliography: p.
   Includes index.
   1. McDougall, Alexander, 1732-1786. 2. Generals—United States—Biography. 3. United States. Army. Continental Army—Biography. 4. Statesmen—United States—Biography. I. Title.
   E207.M12M3   973.3'092'4 [B]   76-15324
   ISBN 0-8371-9035-5

Copyright © 1977 by William L. MacDougall

All rights reserved. No portion of this book may be reproduced, by any process or technique, without the express written consent of the publisher.

Library of Congress Catalog Card Number: 76-15324
ISBN: 0-8371-9035-5

First published in 1977

Greenwood Press, Inc.
51 Riverside Avenue, Westport, Connecticut 06880

Printed in the United States of America

Contents

	Illustrations and Maps	vii
	Foreword by Richard B. Morris	ix
	Preface	xi
	Acknowledgments	xv
1	The Scots Rebel	3
2	"Tell It Not in Boston"	17
3	The Forty-Five Virgins	27
4	Tea and Bloodshed	39
5	Achievement and Disappointment	51
6	Invasion and Tragedy	61
7	The Army Is Saved	75
8	Against the Odds, They Survived	87
9	The Cabal	109
10	In Congress at Last	129
11	An Embarrassing Trial	139
12	Faithful Guardian of His Fame	147
	Appendix	159
	Notes	165
	Bibliography	179
	Index	183

Illustrations and Maps

Alexander McDougall	frontis
The farm where Alexander McDougall was born	7
Pre-Revolutionary cartoon by Pierre Eugène du Simitière showing McDougall's plight during imprisonment in New York's New Gaol	31
Northern military theater	70
Central military theater	93
New York in 1778, a lively city despite the British occupation	117

Foreword

Alexander McDougall is one of the unsung heroes of the American Revolution, and it would be a pity were the Bicentennial to pass without giving him his due. Like Samuel Adams, a principal agitator of the Revolutionary movement, and like Thomas Paine, a flaming penman, if a less gifted one, McDougall chose jail in order to test the liberty of the press and the right of free men to criticize public authority.

As the author of this informed biography reveals, McDougall was one of that new breed of men of humble origins whom the Revolutionary movement propelled forward to seats of power. Sailor, privateersman, and merchant shipper, he had achieved a considerable affluence by the time of the Revolution. Still, even his enemies conceded that he never lost the common touch. To his foes he remained a very common man, for he talked the language of sailors and artisans, a group long excluded from meaningful political power.

To Alexander McDougall there would have seemed nothing inconsistent in his advocating the causes of the common man while at the same time being dedicated to the protection of property rights. Humble in origin, working-class in his early associations, McDougall remained very much the middle class entrepreneur. One should not be surprised, therefore, that, in actively espousing the claims of the unpaid officers of the Revolutionary army, he was prepared to unite their cause with that of the civilian public creditors, nor that he should become a federalist in the postwar years and even a bank president.

As this biography reveals, McDougall's greatest triumphs occurred at the start of the Revolution. Thereafter, despite a solid military career, his contributions were of a lesser order. Other talented men whom he and a small nucleus of radical associates had drawn into the conflict proved more gifted on the field of battle and more creative in statecraft. But Alick McDougall, who more than any single man, nudged New York into the Revolutionary movement, quite appropriately stood in that select company of top officers who embraced Washington at Fraunces' Tavern when at war's end the general delivered his parting remarks.

Historians and the general reader alike will be greatly indebted to the author for restoring Alexander McDougall to his central role among radical agitators, mass organizers, political manipulators, and propagandists of the American Revolution and for showing how his improbable career was not atypical of that group of extraordinary men who in a few brief decades changed the face of history.

Richard B. Morris

Preface

*A*lexander McDougall, a milkman's son who helped to found a nation, blazed across the American Revolutionary scene like a meteor and fell from sight as promptly. Two hundred years later, the slim, fiery-tempered Scotsman whose pen and sword helped to feed the fires of rebellion in his adopted land has all but vanished from the pages of history. Nearly forgotten are his dazzling exploits as the captain of a privateering ship, prosperous New York merchant, provocative essayist whose jail term for libel turned him into a hero in the thirteen colonies, soldier who rose to the highest rank in the American army under General Washington, politician who was a member of the Continental Congress, first and only Minister of the Marine (a post that later became Secretary of the Navy), and financier who became first president of New York's oldest bank.

George Washington, writing to Thomas Jefferson after McDougall's death in 1786, called him a "brave soldier and disinterested patriot" who had been a pillar of the Revolution.[1] The Marquis de Lafayette, who sought his help to mount an invasion of Canada, admiringly called him "the Roman General McDougall."[2] John Adams described him as "a very sensible man, and an open one. He has none of the mean cunning which disgraces so many of my countrymen."[3]

By one account, his outspoken advocacy of independence from British rule was among the main causes of the Revolution. Thomas

Jones, a New York jurist who was forced to flee to England because of his pro-British sentiments, described McDougall as "the principal promoter and encourager of the unhappy disputes which raged with such violence in the colony for many years, terminated in a rebellion, in a dismemberment of the empire, in almost total destruction of thirteen valuable provinces, and in the loss of not less than 100,000 brave men."[4] Jones conceded that McDougall was possessed of "a pretty good genius."

During his jail sentence, which he deliberately chose instead of paying a fine, he continued to publicize the American cause, and, almost overnight, he became the hero of the discontented and the bane of the pro-British establishment. So many New Yorkers called on him in his cell that he began to schedule appointments. The forty-fifth day of his confinement was turned into a virtual holiday for the Whigs, who brought a feast to the jail, including forty-five bottles of Madeira wine and forty-five bottles of ale. Newspapers said the highlight of the day was the arrival at the jail of "forty-five virgins" who joined in the celebration—although one Tory observer grumbled that there was considerable doubt about the right of some of the ladies to claim that distinction.

After his release, McDougall added a new luster to the leadership of the Sons of Liberty, an increasingly revolutionary group to which he helped to recruit such patriots as Alexander Hamilton. Suddenly, he found himself well known in the movement from Massachusetts to the Carolinas, with his name on the lips of all the Committees of Correspondence that were becoming a highly effective colonial "grapevine." They called him "the Wilkes of America"—a reference to an English Member of Parliament who had become a hero to the lower classes and a thorn in the side of the ruling hierarchy.

Although he was not a military genius, McDougall became an able and respected general whose advice repeatedly was sought by Washington, Benjamin Franklin, and General Nathanael Greene. He fought in three major Revolutionary battles—Long Island, White Plains, and Germantown—and commanded West Point for much of the war. Eloquently presenting a soldier's view, he frequently argued before the Congress for better treatment of the army, which more than once threatened to overturn the elected government.

After McDougall's death, the historian Jared Sparks commented that "few men of the Revolution have left a name more worthy."[5] But three decades after that tribute, a lecturer at the New-York Historical Society observed that "the name of Alexander McDougall had become obscure and nigh unto oblivion."

He was a supporting character in the Revolutionary drama, and his descent into the footnotes of history partly reflects the timing of his death, in 1786, too soon after the war's end to have allowed him to contribute much to the organization of the new republic. In a country blessed with more eminent and noteworthy leaders such as Washington, Jefferson, and the Adamses, McDougall's earlier role—important as it was at the time—was quickly forgotten. The exact location of his remains is unknown because his grave apparently was left behind and later razed when the First Presbyterian Church moved in the nineteenth century. About the only visible token of his accomplishments is a short street in New York City named in his honor, and it is misspelled.

This biography is intended to be not only an exploration of those critical times from the viewpoint of one of its earliest contenders, but also a portrait of a colorful, courageous personality who deserves to be remembered.

Acknowledgments

Many people contributed to this book, including John Lawrance Hawkes, great great great grandson of Alexander McDougall, and Mr. Hawkes' wife, Wini, both of whom provided invaluable family documents and offered constant encouragement. Jon Wakelyn was a careful and patient editor. Mrs. Iain Ramsay of the Isle of Islay, Scotland, provided historical expertise about McDougall's birthplace. George Scheer counseled during important phases of the writing. James Gregory of the New-York Historical Society opened the vast store of McDougall Papers at that institution. Sister Anna Madeleine Shannon did pioneering research on McDougall. The Library of Congress, the Huntington Library of San Marino, California; the Rosenbach Foundation of Philadelphia; the New York Public Library; the National Maritime Museum of Greenwich, England; and Union College, Schenectady, New York, also contained valuable documents for research material.

AMERICAN REVOLUTIONARY

The Scots Rebel   1

*I*t was an extraordinary scene in rough-and-tumble New York, a lively port of 20,000 where even in 1740 Indians sometimes brought animal hides for trading, and sailors and workmen often battled it out after long visits to waterfront taverns. A small crowd of men, women, and children, many of them dressed in crude homespun, were arguing and jostling each other on the street, attracting the stares of passersby.

"We didn't leave Scotland to become vassals!" shouted one man.

"And we won't be vassals to Lachlan Campbell in America!" exclaimed another.

Part of the crowd broke away, but the main body moved on, still shouting and arguing, and was joined by others who had just heard the news: Captain Campbell, who had led them to America, was trying to secure a vast estate in the northern part of the Colony of New York on which he would be the laird and they the tenants.[1]

Alarmed by the clamor and fearing outright violence by the quick-tempered Scots, Governor George Clarke hastily summoned some members of the crowd to his chambers, where he patiently listened to their list of grievances. He had been acquainted with Captain Campbell, an ambitious ex-soldier, for several years—since 1737, to be exact. Campbell had come to America to investigate an advertisement by the Colony of New York for "Protestant European immigrants" to settle on the embattled northern frontier, where Indian raids on the white farmers were frequent.[2] The immigrants had been promised 200 acres of unimproved land at little or no charge.

Governor Clarke had urged Campbell to ride north and see the rich, forested expanse near the upper reaches of the Hudson River. Campbell had been as impressed by the countryside as were the local Indians with Campbell, who had come to them dressed in a vivid Scottish Highlands outfit. The Indians were so overwhelmed that they invited him to settle in their midst.

Returning to Scotland, Campbell rode up and down the glens and mountains of his home island, Islay, proclaiming the beauties of America and urging the islanders to follow him to New York. His message fell on fertile ground, for Islay and much of the rest of Argyllshire were feeling the pinch of a fast-growing population which the rocky farms could not support. He recruited eighty-nine families—totaling about 470 people—who sailed to America in three passages in 1738, 1739, and 1740. Many sold most of their possessions to pay for the trip, while others committed themselves to work as indentured servants.

The first group arrived with high hopes in the late summer of 1738 and discovered to their dismay that Captain Campbell had not nailed down all the legal details of his planned "Argyle Patent" of lands, and they could not settle there immediately. Many grumbled, but they had little choice but to wait until the remainder of the group arrived and the legal matters were straightened out.

Most, including Ranald McDougall, a hard-working farmer, gained employment in or near the city, which was fast expanding as a port and trading center. McDougall labored on an outlying farm where he and his wife, Elizabeth, settled with their children: John, Alexander, and Mary, and Elizabeth's illegitimate daughter, Eleanor. They had left Islay in July 1738, with little more than their clothes and a letter from the minister of Kildalton Parish who noted that they "have lived here in said parish and island from their birth, for the most part behaving themselves soberly and honestly and industriously."[3] The minister added that "now that they design for America, I know of no reason why they may not be received into any Christian and civil society there with encouragement." The

McDougalls, like the other Highlanders, were determined to make the most of their opportunities. Shortly before their departure, Ranald and Elizabeth paid a last farewell to three graves of their other children who had not survived childhood.[4]

After the third ship of Islay people arrived in 1740, the ramifications of the Argyle Patent were revealed and the immigrants were enraged. They learned that Captain Campbell had applied to the New York authorities for a huge estate of about 30,000 acres, much of which he was to own and manage. They were to be merely tenants—not landowners, as they had imagined. It was exactly the situation from which they had fled, the rebellious Highlanders told Governor Clarke, and they would not submit to it again in America.

Captain Campbell defended his enterprise, arguing that the estate would benefit the settlers and help to safeguard the colony against Indian attacks. He asked the colonial assembly for financial help in settling the families until they were self-supporting.

His arguments were not convincing enough, however. Cadwallader Colden, the aristocratic lieutenant governor who was prominent in New York for decades, listened to the debate, and concluded that "Captain Campbell had conceived hopes of erecting a lordship for himself in America. He imagined that the people whom he enticed over with him would have become his tenants on condition of being supported till they could maintain themselves and an easy rent afterwards."

Campbell was to be greatly disappointed. The New York Assembly, taking note of "the aversion on which the people who came over with Captain Campbell had to him," refused to approve his petition. The Argyle lands were not to be settled by most of the group for many years, and the Highlanders had to look elsewhere for their fortunes. Some applied for other lands, a few departed for Cuba, and many—such as the Ranald McDougalls—remained in the New York City area.

The controversy was of little interest to most New Yorkers; the episode just another example of cantankerous Scots. Many of the English-American aristocracy considered the Highlanders troublesome and lazy. In fact, Scots were discouraged from settling in Pennsylvania. Much preferred there were the hard-working and cooperative Germans. But the episode was to have far-reaching consequences for all of the immigrants, and for one not yet ten-year-old youngster, in particular. As a result of the Assembly's decision, Alexander McDougall never moved to the wilderness where his parents had intended to raise him. Instead, he grew up on the busy streets of New York, where he would witness and partake in the climax to the struggle between the Old and the New World.

Alick was well acquainted with the city, having helped his father on his delivery route. For a while, Ranald McDougall was indentured to Gerard Beekman, and worked on a farm known as Beekman's Pasture. Contemporaries said Alick often walked along behind his father, "pails on his back, dealing out milk to his father's customers."[5]

New York was especially fascinating to a boy who not long before had never seen anything much larger than a Scottish farm. Manhattan's thoroughfares were lined with fine houses and stores, some with Dutch-style gables and others with white shutters on red brick fronts.[6] The clatter of horses' hooves drawing wagons from the crowded docks was heard from dawn until dusk. Especially fascinating were the Indians who occasionally appeared from their distant retreats to barter for woolen blankets from England and rum from the West Indies.

Even in modest circumstances, the McDougalls were far better off in New York than they had been in Scotland.[7] They had lived on Islay in a "black-house"—a damp, drafty, two-room cottage with stone-and-peat walls and a timber-and-thatched-straw roof with a hole in the center. The opening was intended to let out the smoke from an open cooking fire in the middle of the room, which had only a packed dirt floor, but it didn't always work out that way. Often the smoke from the blaze over which a meal was being prepared settled inside the rooms, making it difficult to breathe. Generally, in such a house, the parents and infant children slept in the bedroom, while the older children shared a bed or two in the combination living room, dining room, and kitchen.

The McDougalls had lived at various times as tenants on two farms, Torrodale and Nether Killean, both of which have long green pastures descending from steep hills to the rocky shores of the North Atlantic. The soil there is shallow, but the grazing is good, and black Highland cattle commanded good prices on the mainland of Scotland. Oats were the main crop grown for the farmers' own

The farm where Alexander McDougall was born, located at the edge of the Atlantic on the Scottish Isle of Islay, in 1732. These buildings were erected later.

tables, and barley was raised for distillation by individual families into whiskey.

The McDougalls, like many other islanders, were intensely religious, and walked about a mile along a hill-sheltered glen at least once every Sunday to the new graystone Church of Scotland on the lands of Ballynaughtonmore farm. The old church had been about six miles away, but the new one was built about the time Alexander was born in midsummer 1732. He was baptized at home, and probably had about a year of schooling at the church, along with other bright children of the parish, before the McDougalls moved to America. The old Scottish "dominies"—ministers—were famed for effective teaching of basic skills in reading, writing, and arithmetic.

Despite their humble circumstances, there was an extraordinary spark about the McDougalls. Even in prior generations, when advanced education was normally reserved for the rich, young impoverished McDougall kinsmen on Islay had been selected because of their native ability to attend school on the mainland. The clan had been noted for its individuality and pugnaciousness since the time of its founding by a Viking prince in the twelfth century.[8] Not many generations before Alexander McDougall, his antecedents had fought battle after bloody battle with rival clans, narrowly escaping wholesale destruction at one time. The Viking royal house from which they were descended is believed to have had an even darker history. Evidence indicates that some Swedish kinsmen who claimed to be descended from the Nordic gods had sacrificed family members in pagan rituals.

All that had long since changed under the sobering influence of the Church of Scotland, but some of the impatience and impetuousness of past generations remained with Ranald McDougall and his brood, who believed they were entitled to a better life than they had on Islay. The island was owned by various Campbells, and land was scarcely if ever for sale. Even if it had been, there was little money except for the proceeds from selling a few cattle in the hands of the islanders. So Lachlan Campbell's expedition to America, with the promise of prosperity for everybody, must have seemed providential to the McDougalls.

For many immigrants who made such a journey, the three- or four-month trip to America was a frightening ordeal. Crowded into tiny, airless spaces below deck where the smell of vomit was inescapable, the passengers suffered from bad food, ill health, and frequent violent storms. Some ships landed after the long crossing with only a fraction of their original group surviving.

The sight of New York harbor must therefore have been a doubly exciting experience for these newcomers. Although New York, Philadelphia, and Boston were the largest cities in the colonies, they were nevertheless small enough so that they appeared from a distance to be only specks of civilization almost hidden by forests and fields. Immigrants reported they could smell the sweet scent of the trees for miles offshore.

There were only about a million colonists in the entire network of English settlements from Maine to Georgia. Most Americans lived in the countryside, the majority in rough-hewn log cabins they had built themselves. They were taming ever-larger expanses with the gun and the plow, lured farther and farther from the protection of the coastlines by cheap and fertile land.

If all had gone as planned, Alick McDougall would have been raised in circumstances such as those, with little access to schools, politics, and wealth. So it was for him a stroke of luck that the Argyle Patents did not work out at that time. Instead, he became a city boy, crossing class barriers through close contact with other members of the Presbyterian Church which was at the center of the lives of most Scottish immigrants and their descendants.

As a teen-ager, Alexander had an uncommon way with words and was regarded as a young man of promise. His father hoped Alick's gift of eloquence would help persuade him to become a minister. It was an ambition which Ranald McDougall had long cherished for himself, but was unable to fulfill because of his poverty and lack of education. Occasionally, as one of the New York church's leading laymen, Ranald would fill in for the absent minister and deliver a sermon to the congregation on Sunday. He was intensely interested in the workings of the church, and became outraged when anyone, including the preacher, was not performing adequately.[9] Religion, he maintained, was a very serious business.[10]

The elder McDougall's increasing dissatisfaction with one minister, the Reverend Pemberton, helped to lead in 1753 to an extraordinary uprising by a sizable part of the congregation who contended that the preacher was neglecting his duties. The critics complained, among other things, that Mr. Pemberton was not making enough house calls to congregation members.

Feeling ran so high that Ranald McDougall and his friend Peter Clarke were deputized by the dissenters to present their case against Mr. Pemberton at a regional meeting of the church in Philadelphia. Eventually, the group forced a reluctant board of trustees at First Presbyterian Church to consider "the measures that had been taken by the restless and unquiet party in the congregation, who had troubled the congregation the last year and had been lately again fomenting divisions."

The dissenters finally had their way, and the church dismissed Mr. Pemberton. It was this kind of tenacity that gave the McDougalls, father and son, a reputation for independence—and trouble-making—in New York.

Alexander, for his part, was devout and well versed in the Bible, and spoke in public with great feeling, although he had a slight stammer. But his aspirations were in a different direction. Itching with ambition, impatient with poverty amid the wealth of New York, he chose a course that may have been in his mind even in his earliest days at Torrodale with its shore on the Atlantic. At the age of fourteen, he signed on to a ship and sailed out of New York harbor to seek a fortune.[11]

It was a hard life for a youngster. The tiny wooden ships which sailed out of New York for ports such as Bristol, Charleston, and Martinique were overcrowded and there was back-breaking work to be done, often for twenty hours a day. Cargo, which included a wide variety of items from half-naked African slaves to freshly cut lumber, had to be loaded and unloaded, sails needed constant attention, and there were endless housekeeping chores. On the longer voyages, meat and vegetables often rotted, but had to be eaten anyway because there was little else to consume until the next port was reached. Disease was a constant danger, and many crews were decimated by smallpox in a matter of days.

McDougall's introduction to the sea came at an especially tempestuous time. The French and English were at war—one of a series of struggles for domination of Europe and the two countries' overseas possessions. Although many Anglo-Americans would have preferred to stay out of King George's War (1745-1748), other hundreds willingly helped British regular forces to penalize the French in North America. In a climax to the war, the French Canadian fortress of Louisbourg on Cape Breton Island was captured by a force of New Englanders,[12] but later handed back to the French. There was also frequent sparring on the seas. In his first year before the mast, he later recalled, he learned that "a superior force at sea, divided in different bottoms, is not equal to two-thirds of it in fewer, because if one or two of the small vessels, on which the force is established, should be disabled, the disparity against that side becomes instantly great. I have seen this position exemplified at the age of 14. . . ."[13]

As a sailor, McDougall was an exceedingly hard worker and rose rapidly through the ranks. His progress was evident, during visits at home, by the quality of his dress, which progressed from tattered trousers and shirts to fashionable, slightly foppish suits, which some wealthier New Yorkers looked down upon as vulgar and ostentatious.

The young sailor took time out at the age of nineteen to return to his native island in Scotland where many of his clansmen still lived.[14] There he fell in love and married a cousin, Ann (Nancy) McDougall. The daughter of a poor but well-educated surveyor, Stephen McDougall, she was three years older than her sailor husband. They lived for a few months on Islay until Alexander decided they must move on to New York. The parish minister sent with them a letter of introduction, observing that the couple had behaved "while residing among us without any offense and modestly and Christianly ."

Stephen McDougall wrote to his son-in-law from Glasgow in March 1752, addressing the letter to Alexander McDougall, "Saylor in New York."[15] The surveyor was apprehensive that Alexander's parents disapproved of his bringing home a penniless bride, but was confident she would win their affections.

In a note to his daughter, Stephen approvingly remarked that Alexander was taking good care of her.[16] He admonished Nancy to "consider how closely by blood you are attached to them, by which there is a double tie on you."

In short order, the couple had three children: John, Ranald Stephen, and Elizabeth.

To support his family, McDougall returned to the sea where his progress was rapid. By the age of twenty-five, he was awarded the command of an eight-gun sloop, *Tyger,* which had a crew of 62.[17] The ship was a "privateer"—a merchant ship armed to protect itself, and, if the opportunity were presented, to attack and seize enemy vessels. France, again, was the enemy, locked in battle with Britain and its colonies for the same reasons which had led to earlier conflicts. This time, in the French and Indian War, the scale of savagery was much greater. Settlement after settlement along the northern and western fringes of the American colonies was burned and pillaged by Indians, encouraged and sometimes led by the French.[18]

On the high seas, too, Frenchmen and Anglo-Americans battled with an almost religious fervor. To augment their regular navies, both Paris and London had authorized merchant ships to take up arms against each other. Privateers roamed the North Atlantic coast from Canada to the Caribbean, where France and England each had prosperous colonies, ripe for plunder.

In such a ship, Captain McDougall set sail from New York in the summer of 1757. His official commissioning papers described the vessel as "bound for a cruise against His Majesty's enemies." *Tyger* and several other privateers rendezvoused off Bermuda, which was a particularly rewarding location because it was not far from a British-owned port and astride the shipping lanes to the French West Indies.[19] The Americans waited there to pounce on any luckless French merchant ship that happened to pass that way, one perhaps that was carrying the usual rich cargoes of sugar, rum, and spices. Each privateer was normally awarded at least a part of the value of any enemy ship it helped to seize—and the prize money was beginning to make many ambitious American sailors rich.

Many unfortunate sailors, however, paid for the adventure with their lives, sometimes at the wrong end of French guns and occasionally at the impartial hands of the elements. McDougall came close to such an end on Sunday, September 4, when, after a few days of eerie calm, a hurricane struck the tiny armada. Towering waves hurtled over the wooden decks, sweeping cargo and at least a few men into the churning water.

Nearby, two other privateers, *Cicero* and *Hester,* also were in trouble. Although the privateers often traveled in packs, they were on their own now as the wind and waves drove them farther and farther apart. Out of sight of the other ships, McDougall ordered desperate measures to save his vessel: cut away the mast and throw overboard four of the heavy guns. Even then, it was touch and go for many hours. The bowsprit was snapped off, and the ship lay on its sides for agonizing moments time after time before righting itself again. It took two days for the storm to abate, at which time McDougall turned his battered little ship to the northwest and home. En route, the crew caught sight of *Cicero* which, despite the loss of a mast, also had managed to survive and continue on its way.

Others were not so lucky. Francis Keffler, commander of the privateer, *Defiance*, accidentally stumbled on the wallowing hull of the sloop, *Fanny*, not far from the island of St. Thomas on January 3 of the following year. The half-starved crew, overjoyed to be rescued, told him their vessel had been devastated by the hurricane on September 5, four months before. Captain Keffler wrote:

> They lost all their sails, mast and every other spar, their roundhouse, rudder, compass, and all their water and provisions, except some flour (part of their cargo) of which they made bread with salt water, and baked it in the sun, on which they lived, with some raw fish that they sometimes struck, for 104 days. They preserved some rain water. . . . It was impossible she could have got safe into any port, and as the people would not continue with her, I took them on board and set her on fire.[20]

Midway in his voyage home, McDougall passed a small English ship, adorned with the carved wooden head of a lion, sailing southeast at daybreak.[21] About an hour later, he spotted a fast schooner, presumably a French privateer, chasing the merchantman. McDougall watched in frustration from a distance as the schooner caught up with the English vessel, which was boarded by the French. Convinced his weakened ship was no match for the Frenchman, McDougall hoisted his square sail and fled at noon when the schooner began to show signs of pursuing *Tyger*. The privateer limped into New York "in a wracked condition" on October 17 to be repaired and refitted.

It was, to his family's regret, only a short visit. Three weeks after his arrival in port, the repairs were completed and *Tyger* was ready to sail.[22]

After farewells at the dock, the captain maneuvered out of the crowded harbor and headed south through the winter seas to the sunshine of the Caribbean. The crew, unfortunately, still had not escaped the misfortunes that had haunted them for weeks. An epidemic of smallpox raced through the vessel in January 1758, leaving the ship's doctor and four of the crew dead.

It was not until late March that McDougall's fortunes finally changed for the better. He wrote from St. Kitts on April 10, 1758, that he had

> brought down a Dutch sloop, as I have been advised to bring all into port that comes from the French islands, as many vessels have been lately condemned here who at first sight apeared to have regular papers, but the fraud was discovered by interrogation. The 17th instant is the day appointed for the condemnation of our pretended Dutch ship, and 'tis the current opinion, not only here but at Martinico and St. Eustatia, that the cargo will certainly be condemned, if not the hull.[23]

McDougall also noted that a companion ship had captured two ships containing valuable cargo.

Although it was a profitable enterprise, it was also extremely dangerous, and McDougall came under pressure from his family to leave the sea and return to New York. While the captain was temporarily living on St. Kitts in August 1758, his father-in-law wrote him to congratulate him on his successes, but added:

> For her (Nancy's) sake and the sake of our dear babies, our grandchildren, cannot help advising you to quit as soon as you have got a sufficient competency to keep you and them comfortable. All the motive we have in this is least any accident should happen you, and if this should be the case, it would touch us as near as if anything should happen any of (our own) two boys.[24]

McDougall temporarily resisted the pressures, however, and was rewarded for his piratical skills with the command of a larger privateer, *General Barrington*, in 1759.[25] The ninety-ton vessel carried a letter of marque (an official commission) from George Thomas, governor of the Leeward Islands. It had a crew of eighty and carried twelve guns. McDougall was then twenty-seven years old.

In mid-June, the vessel made an important catch: the *Saint Esprit*, a French ship sailing out of Martinique.[26] Investigating its papers, McDougall discovered that the ship had previously been called *Prince George*, a British vessel. Captured in passage from Philadelphia, the ship had been recommissioned by the French. McDougall brought the vessel into port at the island of Basseterre for redisposal.

A few months later, after thirteen eventful years at sea, the young captain accepted his family's advice and returned to New York, his privateering days over. With prize money that amounted to a small fortune, he set himself and his family up in style—a style that some New Yorkers considered garish. His clothes, for example, were regarded as outlandish by conservative New Yorkers, who, behind his back, called him a fop. Perhaps it was a reaction to his impoverished childhood that prompted him to proclaim his new-found wealth so ostentatiously. At the same time, he did not neglect his intellectual growth. For the first time in his life, he was able to indulge in the purchase of books, and he built up an extensive library concentrating on history, politics, mathematics, English literature, and military science.

Some acquaintances thought he was putting on airs, and criticized the circumstances surrounding his new affluence. The jurist, Thomas Jones, contemptuously asserted that McDougall had made the bulk of his fortune by exacting "contributions" from innocent Dutch ships.[27] Jones said the captains of those vessels paid their ransom rather than be detained.

Whether or not Jones was right—he was wrong about some other charges—his comments reflected the thinking of a number of other wealthy and well-born New Yorkers who considered McDougall crude and pretentious. A member of the Livingston clan had this to say about McDougall:

> . . . He gets into a privateer, and, suitable to the savageness of his clime and disposition, goes forth a hungry Scotchman as a robber of mankind. . . . He returns home weighty of purse, but unpolished in manner, rough as his profession. Mean as the meanest of [his] race.[28]

If McDougall was ever daunted by such criticism, there is no trace of it in his letters and journals. There was probably no time for much self-pity, if any had been warranted. He was far too busy establishing himself as a merchant.

Although he was not in a class with such wealthy landholders and businessmen as the De Lanceys, Livingstons, and Schuylers, he was, nevertheless, a man of substance who could not be ignored. He was also increasingly active in the Presbyterian Church where he forged social and economic ties with families such as the Livingstons. It was only a matter of time before those ties became political as well—the start of partisan politics in New York where Anglican Tories eventually drew up lines against the Whig dissenters.

"Tell It Not in Boston" 2

There was a deceptive calm over New York and the other American colonies in the innocent first years of the 1760s. Britain had defeated France in the French and Indian War, and, for the first time in years, settlers along the northern frontier of the Colony of New York went to sleep at night without great fear of being scalped in their beds.

In New York City, toasts were drunk to King George III, and London fashions were followed slavishly. Like other colonials from Massachusetts to Georgia, many of the city's residents would have been hard pressed to decide, if it had come to that at that time, whether they were British or American. McDougall evidently felt at home on either side of the Atlantic in this period.

Flushed with success and confident of the future, New York City was fast expanding beyond the southern tip of Manhattan Island. The spires of more than twenty churches dominated the skyline, and a new school, King's College (later to become Columbia University) was already establishing a record of excellence. The John Street Theater often played to full houses, despite the disapproval of some church-goers who believed that the stage was sinful. Sailors from the tall-masted ships in the harbor gathered for relaxation at the grog shops along the waterfront, while merchants and lawyers met for drinks and conversation at such establishments as the elegant Fraunces' Tavern.

The city was, even then, extraordinarily cosmopolitan, populated by English aristocrats and workingmen, French Huguenots who had fled from religious persecution in their homeland, Scots and Irishmen who wanted more than the abject poverty in which they had been born, skilled German tradesmen and artisans, propertied Dutchmen whose forefathers had founded the community, and a large number of Negro slaves.

As the population grew, so did the city environs—steadily northward into the fields and forests between the Hudson and East Rivers. The bustling port was the trading center for New York as well as parts of New Jersey and Connecticut, and ships laden with lumber, furs, and grain carried the region's merchandise to Europe, the West Indies, and Canada, as well as to the other colonies. The vessels returned with such products as fine English china, indigo from the Carolinas, and rum from the Caribbean in a thriving trade that was broadening the base of the city's middle class.

Dominating the southern tip of Manhattan was Fort George, with more than one hundred guns facing the harbor, in the event a French fleet might someday enter the port. The walled fortress had barracks for 200 soldiers who were the resident force of British military headquarters in North America. The post, however, did not seem formidable to New Yorkers, who enjoyed strolling through its grounds past the governor's mansion and gardens. British soldiers and sailors, moreover, were welcome in the churches, homes, and taverns lining the streets.

A surprisingly large variety of churches accommodated such groups as Anglicans, Presbyterians, Lutherans, Moravians, and Quakers. It was important to New Yorkers to know the church to which an acquaintance belonged. The esteemed sons of British nobility and wealthy landowners generally were members of the Church of England. In an increasingly politicized atmosphere, this group took command of much of the power in the city and province, and held it almost until the Revolution. They were often led by the rich and well-connected De Lancey family.

Generally lower on the political scale but increasingly effective were the Scottish merchants, normally Presbyterians, and other

Protestants not so wealthy or socially prominent.[1] This faction, mainly dominated by the Livingston clan, was itself split into conservative and radical divisions. Many followers of this religious and economic grouping eventually formed the nucleus of the Whig party in New York, whose members became the colony's leading revolutionaries. Into this milieu, McDougall, initially uninvolved in politics, was drawn partly because of his contacts within the church. He thus became embroiled in rivalry that was to contribute greatly to the development of the political party system throughout the United States.

In the midst of it all, Alexander McDougall, tall, dapper and good-looking, was tasting the first fruits of success. He had invested well, and his fortune was increasing year by year. His mail-order business, importing and exporting items such as flour, sugar, and lumber to and from the southern colonies, the West Indies and Canada, was prospering.[2] He traveled occasionally to St. Croix to look after his business interests there and to check up on his wife's unreliable brother, William McDougall, who dealt extensively in the slave trade.

To a family which had been so poor, Alick McDougall seemed exceedingly rich, and he often was called upon to help support not only his wife and children but also his mother and father and a variety of relatives. His father-in-law noted with satisfaction that Alick had become a wealthy man, and pointedly complained about the poverty of Scotland: "I think," Stephen McDougall wrote, "you have been very shy with me with respect to the strength of your own circumstances, which I think you need not. For the more you have, the more happy we would be in our thoughts on account of our dear grandchildren, as on your own."

His father-in-law tried to persuade Alick to move his business to the ports of Bristol, England, or Glasgow, but the young captain was not interested.[3] Alick, however, raised the possibility of sending his wife and children to Scotland for an extended visit. Stephen eagerly replied that the cost of maintaining Ann and the three children in Glasgow was not high and he himself would gladly furnish them free rooms in his own large house.

There is no evidence that the McDougall family ever made the long voyage back to Scotland. In one of the great epidemics that swept over the world in the eighteenth century, Nancy McDougall became gravely ill. The captain wrote to his sister-in-law in August 1764: "I need not inform you of the sorrow and loss I have suffered by the loss of my dear Nancy." McDougall was worried about his young daughter, Elizabeth (Betsey), and he observed that "you cannot but be very sensible of how much importance it is to have a daughter's education properly taken care of and directed, and more especially of a motherless one who must, in my present situation, be boarded in another family as I keep no house."[4]

Stephen McDougall replied that he and his wife would gladly undertake to raise their granddaughter.

"Mr. Wilson tells me you are reckoned a very rich man there," the elder McDougall noted. "If so, I hope (you) will not neglect to educate your children well. Do, my dear Alick, send us over little Betsey and trust her education to us in case anything should happen."[5]

Stephen made it clear that "we are in no manner of doubts about your discharging that love and care" toward the children. He was, however, concerned that his religiously inclined son-in-law would force his sons into the pulpit.

"From hence I draw that you will be inclineable to make one or both of my grandsons ministers," Stephen wrote. "If so, I differ widely in opinion, for had I twenty sons, I would not make one of them a minister." Rather, he would prefer his grandsons to be a doctor and a merchant.

As it turned out, there was no cause for alarm. Both boys were enrolled as teen-agers in the College of New Jersey, which became Princeton University.[6] John Alexander McDougall, the captain's older son, was graduated in the class of 1769, and returned to New York to study law. Ranald Stephen McDougall later was to serve as an aide to both his father and General Washington during the Revolutionary War. Captain McDougall, who kept a close watch on all his financial affairs, noted their expenditures carefully, and paid some of their bills by dispatching merchandise ranging from sugar to tar to the "stewart of the colledge."

At the time, McDougall was boarding at the home of the Reverend David Bostwick, a minister from Jamaica who had been engaged by the Presbyterian Church in New York in 1757.[7] McDougall left Betsey in the care of his sister, Mary, who was married to another ship's captain, Alexander Stewart. There was no longer any need for servants of his own, so McDougall arranged for his Negro slave, Colerain, to serve aboard his brother-in-law's ship. McDougall noted: "Capt. Alexander Stewart has rendered me an account of my Negro, Colerain's, wages for the last voyage by which he is indebted to me £18-16-8. Paid insurance for his adventure and policy, £1-16-6."

McDougall also recorded in his "Waste Book" ledger: "Shipped on board the sloop, *William*, Capt. Rodgers, to Pensacola consigned to Evan & James Jones Co. at my risk, a Negro wench, £40."[8]

By 1767, his wealth must have impressed even his father-in-law, with such credits as an account with £4,191 in London; hundreds of pounds sterling owed to him by various businessmen in St. Croix; nearly 3,000 acres of land in Albany County, New York; and other real estate as far away as Wilmington, North Carolina.

There were also personal concerns even closer to his heart. His father-in-law sagely foresaw in 1766 that "as you are yet but a young man, it's natural to suppose you will take another wife. . . ."[9] The following year, Alexander McDougall, at age thirty-five, married his minister's daughter, Hannah Bostwick.

Along with changes in his personal life, McDougall was beginning to become concerned about the growing disputes between America and Britain, particularly about the new taxes that Parliament was introducing. In 1765, the controversy came to a head with the Stamp Act, which Britain viewed as a means of forcing the colonies to pay for part of the debts incurred in the French and Indian War. Because a major effect of that conflict had been to secure peace for the colonies, many Members of Parliament reasoned that the Americans ought to be grateful for their security. They weren't—at least not to the extent of having their taxes raised.

Often divided in the past, the colonial legislatures rose in wrath against a tax that was to be levied on Americans alone. One of the taxes was in the form of stamps on licenses, legal papers, and publications. Stamp officers were appointed to collect duties, but in city after city, they were threatened and manhandled, and often prevented from carrying out their assignments.

The New York radicals were deprived of the opportunity of harrassing their own stamp master, who quickly resigned. But they had secondhand revenge on London when Zacharias Hood, the British stamp master of Maryland, was hounded out of that colony, and fled to New York. Residents of the city soon discovered his identity, and angry patriots threatened him. Ill with fever and refused lodging, he sought help from Acting Governor Colden. A room was found for him at Fort George, but even there, the radicals pursued him. The luckless fellow was finally given refuge at Colden's farm on Long Island, and he soon faded from public attention.

In Massachusetts, a call was sounded for a Stamp Act Congress to see what could be done. Representatives of nine colonies met in New York and issued a denunciation of the law, asserting that Americans should not be subject to acts which did not affect all Englishmen. A group of New York merchants, in the same spirit, agreed on October 31, 1765, not to import merchandise from England until the Stamp Act was repealed.

The next night, several thousand New Yorkers, mostly sailors, laborers, and the lower-class workers, gathered in the streets to protest the tax.[10] Bearing a paper effigy of the governor, they approached high-walled Fort George at the tip of the harbor where a contingent of British soldiers was stationed. The crowd singled out a Major James for verbal abuse. He had threatened to "cram the stamps down their throats" with his sword if necessary. The mob challenged Major James to give orders to fire, but he declined. The crowd took out its fury on the officer's home, where they destroyed windows, doors, looking glasses, mahogany tables, silk curtains, a library, and all the china.

The civil authorities defused the trouble by promising not to impose the taxes immediately. The mob, placated, broke up and returned to their homes.

Many in Parliament were shocked by the violence that occurred not only in New York but in several other cities. Some considered the incidents a direct challenge to their authority. A few, however, sympathized with the colonists. Among them was Colonel Isaac Barré, a veteran of the Canadian campaign in the French and Indian War, who knew the colonies well. In a speech in Parliament, Colonel Barré charged that America had prospered despite the neglect of Britain, and added:

> As soon as you began to care about them, that care was exercised in sending persons to rule them in one department or another, who were perhaps the deputies of deputies to some mem-

bers of this house, sent to spy out their liberties, to misrepresent their actions, and to prey upon them; men whose behavior on many occasions has caused the blood of those Sons of Liberty to recoil within them.[11]

Colonel Barré concluded that ". . . the same spirit of freedom which actuated that people at first will accompany them still."
The officer's stirring words might have gone unnoticed in the colonies except for Jared Ingersoll, an agent for the Province of Connecticut. He took notes during Barré's speech, and forwarded a report on it to friends at home. At about the same time that Patrick Henry was denouncing the Stamp Act in the Virginia House of Burgesses, Ingersoll's message was printed in a New London newspaper. Other colonial presses reprinted the speech, and Barré's warning rallied radical opinion from Boston to Charleston. Almost immediately radicals throughout the colonies began to call themselves the "Sons of Liberty."
At first rather formless and disorganized, the group vented its anger against the British in protest meetings, oratory, essays, and occasional outbursts of violence. Many of its early members were from lower classes. Some rowdies used the cause as an excuse to rob private homes and terrorize innocent people, and the "Sons of Liberty" were viewed with disgust by many respectable Americans.
But the ranks also included such responsible individuals as members of the Livingston and De Lancey families, John Morin Scott (an eminent lawyer), Captain Isaac Sears (a former privateer who had become a merchant), and his friend and fellow ex-sailor, Alexander McDougall.[12] McDougall had his own financial interests at heart, because he and the other merchants had been hurt by the new laws. But he was also motivated by a sense of indignation over what he regarded as English tyranny.

"Has not our Mother Country, by solemn act of legislation, declared that she has a right to impose internal taxes on us?" he wrote. "And is not such an imposition incompatible with our liberty? . . . Amidst all the disparity of fortune and honors, there is one lot as common to all Englishmen as death. It is that we are all equally free."[13]

Under pressure from hard-hit English businessmen who wanted

to revive trade with the colonies, Parliament reconsidered its action, and the Stamp Act was repealed in 1766. When the news reached America, the New York Sons of Liberty took to the streets again— this time in a boisterous victory celebration. Bells rang all over New York, a twenty-one gun salute was fired, and huge bonfires were lighted. As a symbol of their achievement, the Sons of Liberty erected a wooden pole, which they called a Liberty Pole, in the Fields—now City Hall Park. It was tantalizingly within view of the British troops at Fort George, and immediately became the focal point of drunken tussles between the citizens and soldiers, who cut it down several times. As often as it was felled, the pole was re-erected by the patriots.

The jubilation in the streets of New York, Boston, Charleston, and Philadelphia was not to last long. Another law, the Mutiny Act of 1765, was still in force, which gave British officers in America the right to house their soldiers in private homes. When Americans objected, arguing that it would imperil the chastity of their daughters, the act was amended to provide for the quartering of troops in empty houses. But the legislation also required the colonies to pay for a considerable portion of the costs of maintaining the soldiers, and it soon became clear to the Americans that they had gained little in their confrontation over the Stamp Act. Parliament, in which the colonials had no representatives, was still in control and could impose taxes on the Americans if it wanted to do so.

The colonies reacted as expected. In 1766, the Massachusetts House of Representatives refused to provide supplies for the soldiers. Legislators in New York, claiming that the Mutiny Act was unconstitutional, skirted part of the act while abiding by other provisions. But even that compromise was not enough for London, which sniffed rebellion in the wind. The New York Assembly was suspended until it would comply fully with the law. The colonies also were faced with new taxes on such items as glass, paper, and tea. Resistance to the tea tax soon became the rallying cry of the American patriots, with the Sons of Liberty leading the way. Following the example of the merchants of Boston, New York's principal businessmen met at Fraunces' Tavern in 1768 and agreed not to import British goods.[14] Events were building up to the same kind of crisis atmosphere that had been caused by the Stamp Act.

In New York, rivalry was growing in the Assembly between the De Lancey and Livingston factions. McDougall had campaigned in a prior election for the Livingstons, but his efforts were unsuccessful. The De Lanceys gained clear control of the Assembly. Searching for an issue on which to engineer their overturn of the De Lancey group, the Livingston organization found just what they were looking for in the controversy over quartering troops. The De Lanceys made it clear they would agree to London's demands in order to keep the peace. While debate was going on in the Assembly, members of the Sons of Liberty, including McDougall, sat watching the session in silent fury. Minority leaders, such as the young lawyer George Clinton, who was friendly with McDougall, protested but to no avail. The patriots agreed it was time for action.

McDougall returned to his home, where he spent about two days composing an angry essay entitled, "To the Betrayed Inhabitants of the City and Colony of New York."[15] (For the text of this broadsheet, see the Appendix.) A ringing denunciation of the Assembly, the paper was so inflammatory, McDougall realized, that it would be less risky to publish it anonymously. He took the composition to a printer, James Parker, and ordered several hundred copies made.

On the night of December 16, 1769, the broadsheets were posted on walls over a large part of the city. The task was performed surreptitiously and ingeniously by an unidentified man who carried a large box.[16] Concealed inside were the posters and a small boy. The man would stop as if to rest, lean the box against a wall, and the boy would draw back a sliding panel and paste the broadsheet to the building. They did this time after time until the distribution was complete.

Mayor Whitehead Hicks, who was one of the first to see the poster, could hardly believe his eyes. The message read:

> In a day when the minions of tyranny and despotism in the mother country and the colonies are indefatigable in laying every snare that their malevolent and corrupt hearts can suggest to enslave a free people. . . . It might justly be expected that . . . the representatives of this Colony would not be so hardy nor be so lost to

all sense of duty to their constituents (especially after the laudable example of the Colonies of Massachusetts Bay and South Carolina before them) as to betray the trust committed to them.[17]

But that, McDougall charged, was exactly what the Assembly had done. The legislators, according to the paper, had acted villainously in appropriating money for the support of British troops who were in America "not to protect but to enslave us." The author argued that Parliament would interpret the vote as "deserting the American cause." He also attacked the De Lancey family and Lieutenant Governor Colden for encouraging the vote for personal gains "to secure to them the sovereign lordship of this colony"—at least slightly reminiscent of the charge brought by Colden against Captain Campbell years before. Calling for a meeting to oppose the Assembly's action, McDougall continued: "And will you suffer your liberties to be torn from you by your representatives? Tell it not in Boston; publish it not in the streets of Charles-Town! You have means yet left to preserve a unanimity with the brave Bostonians and Carolinians; and to prevent the accomplishment of the designs of tyrants."

The paper was signed, "A SON OF LIBERTY."

The broadsheet caused an immediate sensation. The De Lancey faction was horrified that they should be charged publicly with selling out fellow citizens and that the charge was so widely believed. Although at first some Tories believed the broadsheet was so irresponsible that it should be ignored, it quickly became apparent by widespread gossip on the streets that the message had struck a spark. The Tories became alarmed, while the Sons of Liberty were pleased. The paper was hastily dispatched to the patriots' Committees of Correspondence in other colonies, and was widely quoted and reproduced.

McDougall had acted partly out of loyalty to the Livingstons. But, more than anything else, he was expressing his Calvinist conscience and belief in the rights of free men. As much as anything he was ever to do, the publication was to bring him fame and abuse on a national scale—catapulting him to the front ranks of America's emerging revolutionaries.

The Forty-Five Virgins 3

*W*ithin hours of McDougall's anonymous call for a meeting to protest the Assembly's vote, 1,400 angry New Yorkers converged on the Fields.[1] There, in a tumultuous session, they drew up a statement of opposition to the legislature's action, and elected John Lamb, a liquor merchant, as chairman of the gathering. They voted overwhelmingly against offering pay to the British troops, and presented their resolution to the city's representatives in the legislature. The Tories, following the advice of James De Lancey, brushed their demands aside.

The city was in an uproar and spoiling for a fight. Within days after the meeting in the Fields, British soldiers attacked the Liberty Pole, unsuccessfully attempting to blow it up. A small group of patrons at nearby Montayne's Tavern, which was a favorite Sons of Liberty meeting place, ran out to protest, but were repelled by the soldiers. The tavern was wrecked. Two nights later, the pole was destroyed, broken into pieces, and strewn in front of the tavern.

On the following day, 3,000 people converged again on the Fields to express their outrage.[2] They overwhelmingly voted for resolutions declaring "enemies to the peace of the city all soldiers below the rank of orderly who appeared armed in the streets, and all, armed and unarmed, who were found out of barracks after roll call."

The troops retaliated the next day by posting placards throughout the city which charged that the Sons of Liberty were responsible the trouble. Isaac Sears and another Son of Liberty, Isaac Quackenbos, caught three soldiers in the act of distributing the papers, and forced them to march to the office of Mayor Hicks. The action that followed became known as the "Battle of Golden Hill."[3]

The procession to the mayor's office attracted about twenty soldiers and a group of Americans, who squared off against each other—the troops armed with swords and bayonets and the civilians with clubs and stakes. In an attempt to prevent trouble, Mayor Hicks ordered the soldiers to return to their barracks. They obediently set out for the fort, followed by the jeering New Yorkers. Along the way, in an area of John Street called Golden Hill (where fields with golden grain had once stood) another group of soldiers rushed up behind the Americans. A man standing in a doorway was badly wounded, and an elderly sailor was fatally slashed by a sword or bayonet. A woman who opened her door to admit an injured boy narrowly avoided being cut down herself by a bayonet thrust. A group of officers arrived at last, and shouted orders for the men to return to their barracks. They did, but outbursts of fighting continued for some time.

The New York historian, Hugh Hastings, noted later that the battle preceded the Boston Massacre by two months.[4] "The average American historian ignores or rarely mentions Golden Hill," he commented, "but devotes several pages or a chapter to the Boston Massacre, which, in importance, the results that followed, and the effects produced upon the minds of the patriots in other colonies fails to rank as high as the struggle on Golden Hill."

The battle resulted in an even more volatile colony, and the authorities were determined to end such commotion.[5] There was, in the view of the conservatives, good reason to make an example of the upstart, McDougall. The radical Sons of Liberty, egged on by the two ex-privateers, McDougall and Sears, were challenging the very heart of the system that had kept New York's aristocracy in power. Disgusted by what they regarded as a home-grown tyranny ruling the masses by intimidation, the radicals proposed such measures as elections by ballot instead of by voice vote, which everybody knew could be manipulated by those already in power.

When the proposal came up before the colonial legislature, it was quickly voted down. The De Lancey party was convinced that a showdown with the Sons of Liberty was inevitable, and that the broadsheet attack on the Legislature was more than adequate grounds for retaliation.

Many conservatives immediately suspected McDougall of having written the tract because he had recently been voicing similar sentiments privately. They agreed, however, that in order to prove their case against him they must operate within the law. Hence a £100 reward was offered for information leading to the discovery of the author.

Attracted by the money, Michael Cummins, a young apprentice printer from Cork, Ireland, identified his boss, James Parker, as the man who had printed the posters.[6] On February 7, 1770, Parker was taken into custody and detained at the fort. He at first denied that he knew who the author was, but when the authorities threatened him with a long jail term and the loss of valuable government contracts, he spoke. After securing a promise that he would not be prosecuted, Parker identified McDougall as the author. The following morning, McDougall was arrested at his home and charged with causing a "false, seditious, and infamous libel" to be printed. He was conducted to Chief Justice Daniel Horsmanden's chambers and apprised of the seriousness of the situation. McDougall recalled:

> His honor said to me, "So you have brought yourself into a pretty scrape."
>
> To which I replied, "May it please your honor, that must be judged by my peers." He then told me that there was full proof that I was the author or "publisher of the above mentioned paper" which he called a false, vile, and scandalous libel. I replied again, "This must also be tried by my peers."
>
> His honor thereupon informed me that I must either give bail or go to jail. I answered, "Sir, I will give no bail."

McDougall was then led off to the New Gaol (jail).

The authorities were amazed that he had chosen imprisonment instead of paying the bail which he easily could have afforded. They were convinced he did it to become a martyr—to focus attention on himself and harass the establishment. From his own standpoint, the action accomplished three things: it satisfied his need for an expression of outrage against "tyranny," rallied support for the libertarian cause, and brought pressure on civil authorities to lift the measures that had hurt his business.

News of his arrest electrified the radicals, who perceived, as McDougall did, that his detention would win them sympathy. His supporters rallied to his side. McDougall himself went into action, dispatching a flood of letters to the newspapers and patriotic groups. Committees of Correspondence, in turn, took up his cause in the other colonial cities. The captain made it clear that he was protesting against what he considered an ill-advised act of the local legislature, and not against the "gracious King upon the throne."[7] He concluded one letter to a New York newspaper with the observation that "Americans may enjoy British liberties and British securities to the latest posterity is the ardent prayer and (when delivered from his imprisonment) shall be the strenuous endeavors of the public's most obedient humble servant, Alex. McDougall."

The New York Sons of Liberty considered McDougall's plight similar to that of the English editor and legislator, John Wilkes, who had sided with the masses on various issues and made himself thoroughly unpopular with the leaders of Parliament.[8]

The conservatives, on the other hand, were thoroughly alarmed by the increasingly ugly mood of the city. They rose to the support of Governor Colden, as they had often refused to do in less troubled times. Only about fifteen of the seventy-three Chamber of Commerce members, it was said, supported their fellow merchant, McDougall.[9] The majority was described as considering him an "empty, insignificant, self-conceited im-p-t body" who wasn't even capable of composing the broadsheet.[10]

Colden complained that McDougall was imitating Wilkes in every way possible. The official observed that most respectable people in New York openly say that McDougall "highly deserves punishment."[11]

Even McDougall must have been amazed and delighted by the

The Forty-Five Virgins 31

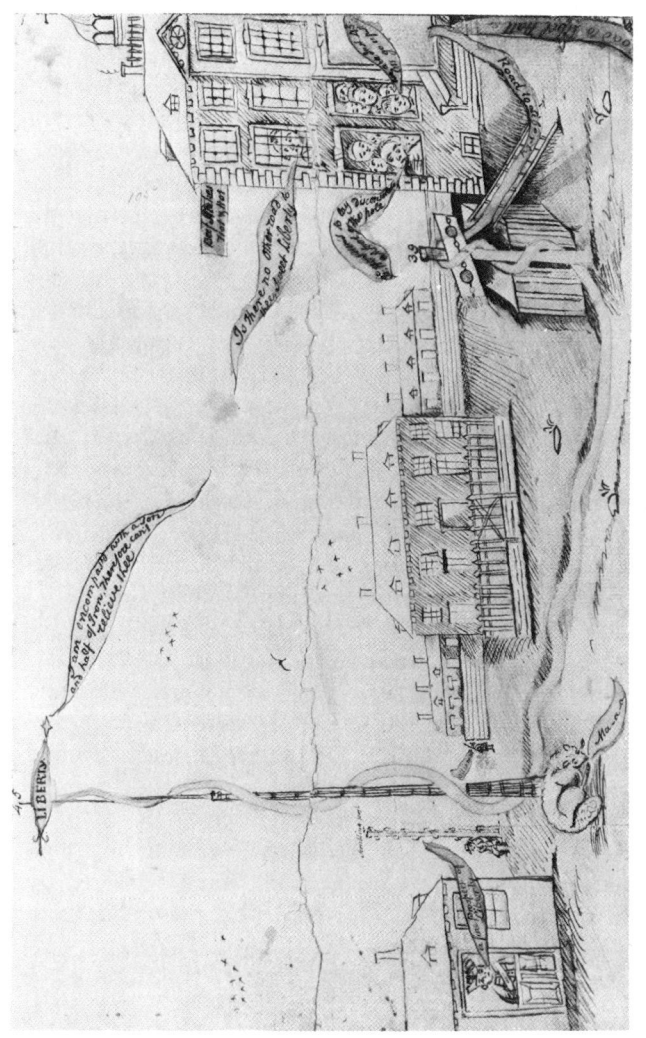

Pre-Revolutionary cartoon by Pierre Eugène du Simitière showing McDougall's plight during imprisonment in New York's New Gaol (right). Presumably McDougall is the face in second-story window gazing at the Liberty Pole and lamenting: "Is there no other road to thee, Sweet Liberty."

furor his imprisonment was causing. Intellectuals, who had had no reason to pay attention to McDougall before, suddenly found him the primary topic of the city. Writers flocked to his cell, and newspapers were filled with debate over his case. One artist, Pierre Eugène du Simitière, captured the spirit of the radicals at that moment with a cartoon that depicted the tortuous turns that the road to liberty had taken.[12] To the right of the commons, a green stretch of park, stood the three-story jail with a tower on top. In a second-story window, a solitary figure—presumably McDougall—is staring across the commons at the liberty pole, and saying: "Is there no other road to thee, Sweet Liberty." The jail is labeled by the artist as "Libel Hall."

The event also stirred debate in many of America's leading newspapers, and culminated in a remarkable series of essays called "Dougliads," denouncing the captain. The series, in turn, provoked letters of defense by McDougall's friends. The merchant was hailed as "undoubtedly a gentleman and universally esteemed as a truly great man; his endowments are great, and exceedingly well cultivated, and is fixed firm as a rock in the grand and sacred cause of liberty."[13]

The anonymous author of the Dougliads, on the other hand, compared McDougall with various historical villains, and commented with heavy sarcasm: "How immensely, then, are we indebted to our American champion for his patriotic and seasonable address to the betrayed inhabitants of this city and colony!" The writer added that McDougall's essay was "calculated to blind and seduce, to distract and disunite, to foment discontent, tumults and sedition, and, in short, to trample down all legal authority and shake the government to the foundation.[14]

The criticism, which continued in the same vein for many weeks in the *New York Gazette,* was followed by a note from the printer informing McDougall that "should he think himself injured by anything that may be inserted in this paper, his press is open to him for a reply."

In a later issue, a defender of McDougall retorted that

> . . . the ungenteel and inhuman treatment of our patriot prisoner, Captain McDougall, appears beyond the power of description. The rude and malicious writings and publications of some of the

New York Tories against him (particularly that of the Dougliad No. 1) are scarce to be equalled in all the volumes of history. (The Dougliad is an amazing stab, indeed; we may certainly conclude that piece was intended as one of the deepest stabs to the liberties, to the Sons of Liberties in America, etc., that ever was published from any press on the continent.)[15]

The correspondent also lambasted the Dougliad for vilifying "a prisoner of unblemished reputation, and that before he is legally adjuged by his peers, guilty or not guilty."

McDougall's reply to such criticism was that he was willing to stand up to the "star chamber of libels" which John Peter Zenger had faced some twenty-five years earlier. In a landmark decision for American journalism, Zenger had been acquitted by establishing truth as a defense for the "libel" of which he was accused. McDougall took pride in becoming one of the first Americans to be imprisoned in defense of freedom of the press.

"I rejoice," he explained, "I am the first sufferer for liberty since the commencement of our glorious struggles. . . ." McDougall added that he would cherish his imprisonment if it promoted the cause of liberty. Martyrdom clearly was to his liking.[16]

The prisoner, who suddenly found himself at center stage not only in New York but also in the other colonies, was interviewed in his cell day after day by dozens of supporters. To maintain some order, he began to schedule appointments, usually confining most calls to the afternoon. A Philadelphia newspaper, which published a lengthy biography of the newly discovered patriot hero, said McDougall possessed "great presence of mind, is methodical, and connected in the arrangement of his ideas, writes well, speaks (though with some impediment) yet with tolerable ease. Has great fire and vehemence. . . ." The writer described the captain as "powerfully supported," and concluded that "his enemies will find in the end that they have a bear by the tail."[17]

The De Lancey faction, which at first thought it had the situation well in hand, became increasingly worried. Some of the group believed they should try to defeat the radicals at their own game. The Tories rented Montayne's Tavern, which had been the center of activity for the Sons of Liberty, for a banquet to observe the anniversary of the end of the Stamp Act. By doing so, they thought, they could appropriate for themselves the laurels, if not the name itself, of the Sons of Liberty.

The more ardent patriots, however, who would have nothing to do with the Tories, bought a small, one-story structure near the Liberty Pole. The radicals named their unassuming building Hampden Hall, which they publicly proclaimed as headquarters for the true Sons of Liberty.

On February 14, supporters of "the American Wilkes" arranged a celebration to mark the forty-fifth day of the year—symbolic of the forty-fifth issue of John Wilkes's newspaper, the *North Briton,* which contained a libel that led to the Englishman's imprisonment.[18]

A Boston newspaper reported that "forty-five gentlemen, real enemies to internal taxation by, or in obedience to external authority, and cordial friends of American liberty, went in decent procession to the New Gaol; and dined with him [McDougall], on forty-five pounds of beef steaks, cut from a bullock of forty-five months old." A highlight of the evening was the arrival of forty-five "virgins," described as "female lovers of liberty," who sang forty-five songs.

The occasion was ridiculed by the Tories, who sarcastically observed that McDougall who "is courted in a gloomy prison by forty-five (virgins) in one day cannot fail of being a man indeed."

In a mock tribute to the vigorous young captain, the author of the Dougliads wrote:

> Let men admire, virgins sing, and matrons mumble thy exalted virtues! . . . A dreary prison is, in his estimation, the paradise of Mahomet, graced with forty-five black-eyed virgins who are continually caressing him. . . .

McDougall happily put up with all such mock praise, but complained that it was a low blow when his critics had commented in print that the forty-five "virgins" were all forty-five years old.

While awaiting a grand jury hearing, McDougall consulted with his admirers and publicized his cause in the American press. Many New Yorkers were disillusioned with the colonial Assembly, which was widely regarded as merely a tool of the aristocratic De Lancey faction and uninterested in the rights of the common man. It was generally expected that the De Lancey group would try to pack the grand jury with men sympathetic to their side, and so the opposing Whigs attempted to take countermeasures. Isaac Sears, known as "King Sears" for his radical leadership, wanted to be a jurist and tried to persuade Sheriff John Roberts to appoint him. Whigs from New England and Pennsylvania also indicated they would descend en masse on New York to exert pressure on the court.

In the words of one Tory, the final jury consisted entirely of "the most impartial, reputable, opulent, and substantial gentlemen in the city," none of them McDougall supporters.[19] Virtually all parties predicted from the start that their verdict would be against the captain.

John Carr, a printer, testified that he did not know for certain who had written the plea "to the betrayed inhabitants."[20] He had, however, seen Captain McDougall in Mr. Parker's print shop, and noticed that the ex-sailor had taken a pen and corrected "a word or letter" in the paper. He also observed that McDougall "came some time after and took away some of the papers." Carr noted that he could not verify whether the original manuscript had been in McDougall's handwriting. The manuscript had disappeared some time before the authorities searched Parker's shop and McDougall's home. Three other witnesses offered similar testimony, with none of them able to identify McDougall as the author. The court records unaccountably indicate that the chief witness, Parker, did not testify.

On April 25, despite flimsy evidence, the jurors decided against McDougall, and declared him to be a "person of turbulent and unquiet mind and seditious disposition" who had brought "the utmost hatred, scandal, distrust, and contempt" upon the Assembly. He was ordered to prepare himself for a full trial.[21]

The court, however, was approaching the end of its term, and the captain was advised that the trial would probably not be held until late in the year. McDougall's friends, "being satisfied his confinement must be grievous and oppressive, procured bail for his appearance" and he was freed after nearly three months of imprisonment.

The Sons of Liberty, who were not above rigging justice, decided to take matters into their own hands. Recognizing that the Crown's case depended on the printers' testimonies, the patriots distributed handbills threatening that the printers would be tarred and feathered and turned over to the Sons of Liberty for further punishment. One printer went into hiding, and then fled to Boston and later to England.[22] Parker escaped the patriots' wrath because he was considered sympathetic to their side. However, in midsummer, on a trip to New Jersey, he died after having suffered for some time from ill health. The Tories, though, claimed his death was "not without strong suspicions of foul play."

Even though the case against McDougall appeared to have withered, the colonial Assembly still wanted its vengeance. In December, the captain was summoned to the bar of the legislature where the case reopened.[23]

Standing in front of the lawmakers, McDougall was advised by the speaker that he was charged with having written the infamous document. By order of the House, the captain was commanded to state whether or not he was guilty.

McDougall, uncowed, demanded instead to confront his accusers.

The speaker, Mr. De Noyellis, ordered McDougall not to talk until he had asked permission of the House. The prisoner tried again to speak, and was warned to keep silent or face a motion of contempt. One lawmaker declared that he had no doubt that McDougall had written the paper.

George Clinton[24] rose and said he presumed it was not the intention of the House to prevent the accused from replying so long as he treated the Assembly with "decency and respect." The legislators then allowed the merchant to speak.

McDougall protested that the charge against him was too indefinite, and refused to state whether he had written the broadsheet. He said he could not answer a question that might impeach him.

That was too much for De Noyellis. He demanded that McDougall be compelled to answer. Clinton, however, argued that the House had the power to throw McDougall "over the bar or out of the windows, but that the public would be the judge of the justice of it." He also claimed there was not enough information available.

The climax came on the final day of the captain's appearance before the legislature. McDougall vividly described the scene: ". . . The malevolent say that the second day I went to the House, I laughed and took snuff in derision and contempt of the members, for which I was committed." This statement was untrue, he said, maintaining that he had been "very circumspect" in his conduct. He insisted he had not given any sign of contempt of the House, resisting the inclination even to smile.

"Others with as little truth say that I doubled my fist at the House, and knocked on the speaker's desk, for which I was committed," he reported. "The former is misrepresented, and the latter is not true. I suppose it alludes to my raising my hand, which was an action pertinent to what I was going to say when I told Mr. Speaker: 'That rather than resign the rights and privileges of a British subject, I would suffer my right hand to be cut off at the bar of this House.'"[25]

As he knew in advance, there was little sympathy for him in the Assembly, and the lawmakers overwhelmingly declared him guilty of contempt. The Assembly demanded that he ask for their pardon, but he refused to do so. Ordered into custody for his stubbornness, McDougall, to the consternation of the members, at first put up a fight. But he eventually submitted and was led to the New Gaol for the second time that year. He remained there several weeks, occasionally firing off broadsheets and letters to his supporters. One such paper concluded: "For the many visits I have received from my friends of all ranks, I am affected with sincere gratitude. They may rest assured that none of their rights shall be silently resigned. . . ."

Soon afterward, the authorities reluctantly became convinced that they had no real case against McDougall and released him. He walked out of prison a second time, cheered by the greetings of friends.

The results were mixed. McDougall's imprisonment had made no real effect in the Assembly, where he was despised by the majority. But it did gain him a cachet among a steadily growing number of patriots. In addition to his New York colleagues, his circle of friends grew to include future presidents of the United States and other eminent Americans. He corresponded with all the leaders of the patriotic cause, and his advice was welcomed in the best of circles—even, on occasion, in the corridors of Parliament in London.

One of his new friends was Benjamin Franklin, the inventor, printer, and sage from Philadelphia. McDougall corresponded frequently with Franklin, who was in London serving as a colonial agent, a lobbyist who represented American interests in dealings with the British government.[26]

Franklin wrote to McDougall in March 1770 that the New Yorker's "very judicious" views had been circulated among members of Parliament, and "had due weight with several. You will see that I printed it at length in the London *Chronicle*."[27]

Despite McDougall's timely assistance, however, Franklin noted that he had been unable to persuade Parliament to repeal the taxes that had brought about the nonimportation agreements in America. Some members, Franklin said, had been influenced by "lying letters said to be from Boston that the associations not to import were all breaking to pieces, that America was in the greatest distress for want of goods, that we could not possibly subsist any longer without them, and must of course submit to any terms Parliament should think fit to impose on us."

Franklin warned there was a faction in Parliament that "never speak of us but with evident malice. Rebels and traitors are the best names they can afford us, and I only believe they wish for a colorable presence and occasion of ordering the soldiers to make a massacre among us."

At the same time, the Philadelphian informed McDougall, "we have for sincere friends and well-wishers the body of dissenters generally throughout England, with many others not to mention Ireland and all the rest of Europe, who from various motives join at applauding the spirit of liberty. . . ." Urging his fellow Americans to continue their resistance, Franklin concluded: ". . . There is no doubt that if we are steady and persevere in our resolutions, these people will soon begin a clamor that much pains has hitherto been used to stifle."

As these and other communications from patriot leaders indicate, McDougall had become a highly regarded leader in the revolutionary movement.

Never again would the colonial authorities, who not long before had dismissed him as unimportant, fail to take him, his followers, and their cause seriously.

Tea and Bloodshed 4

As a reflection of the great divisions in the American colonies in the 1770s, revolutionary fervor ebbed and flowed across the continent like the tides of trade associated so closely with the movement.

In Boston, where patriotic feeling was especially intense, British troops were needed to keep the heated revolutionaries quieted. At issue there and elsewhere was whether agreements not to import British goods should be enforced. Boston already had a bad reputation in England for the way it had treated stamp masters and customs collectors during the Stamp Act disorders—when they were forced to flee for their lives. Later, the British garrison was cut in half, and the radicals were able to take out their wrath on the remaining soldiers. The redcoats were accused of rape and beatings, and the soldiers, often without provocation, were assaulted in the streets by angry and drunken citizens.

In the aftermath of one such incident in which a redcoat was seriously injured, a surly crowd advanced on the sentry at the customs house. An alarmed officer rounded up a force of armed men and confronted the mob. He tried at first to discuss the situation with them, but the shouting townspeople marched to the edge of the soldiers' bayonets, which had been leveled at the crowd. A redcoat was knocked down, and the soldiers began firing into the mob.

Amid screams and shouts, the citizens halted, but five of their group already were dead or dying. The incident ended when the soldiers retreated to their barracks, and the crowd collected the victims.

News of the "Boston Massacre" spread rapidly through the colonies, but the results were not entirely what the radicals expected. They, not the British, were widely blamed by many moderates for creating the incident to advance their cause.

In the large ports, including New York, the merchants pointed to the battle as an example of what could be expected if the Sons of Liberty gained power. The episode also gave the businessmen, whose firms were suffering from the lack of trade with London, the occasion to call for an end to nonimportation. The policy had worked exceedingly well in New York, with imports falling to a fraction of what they had been a few years earlier. The price of items such as china climbed enormously; some materials such as nails were scarce; and unemployment soared.

It was time, the majority of merchants decided, to put an end to the nonsense. Learning that Newport, Rhode Island, already had renewed trade with Britain, New York businessmen—McDougall excepted—waged a concerted campaign to take the same action. The Sons of Liberty were equally determined to maintain nonimportation of British goods. At a mass meeting, radical New Yorkers condemned Newport for its weakness, and informed merchants that anyone who refused to abide by nonimportation would be considered an enemy.

Many New York storekeepers, however, adamantly wanted to resume business as usual. They first attempted to rally fellow merchants in other cities to their side by proposing a regional meeting in Connecticut to reach a determination that would affect all areas jointly.[1] Connecticut and New Jersey businessmen scoffed at the idea, so the proposal was abandoned.[2]

Subsequent tactics adopted by the New York conservatives were more successful. They suggested that a city poll be taken to determine popular sentiment. By carefully restricting their efforts to the city's 1,200 wealthiest citizens, the group easily obtained a "majority" who favored a resumption of trade. The Sons of Liberty called the poll dishonest, but the elated merchants claimed they were following the will of the people and pronounced the end of nonimportation. The announcement was greeted with rage from the city's radicals and a considerable degree of resentment from businessmen in other cities such as Boston and Philadelphia who claimed the New Yorkers had broken faith.

In a broadsheet "To the Free and Loyal Inhabitants of the City and Colony of New York," "Brutus"—a pseudonym often used by McDougall—railed against his fellow "mercantile dons" for attempting to prevent others from expressing their views about the trade ban.[3] "Brutus" thundered: "When the nonimportation agreement took place, what end was it designed to answer? Not, surely, the private emolument of merchants, but the universal weal of the Continent."

"Brutus" urged New Yorkers to resist the temptation to return to trading with Britain when Parliament had infringed upon the liberties of Americans. He declared:

> Rouse, then, my fellow citizens, fellow countrymen, and fellow freemen of all ranks, from the man of wealth to the man whose only portion is liberty. Suffer not a few interested, parricidal and treacherous inhabitants to gratify their avarice at the expense of our common interests.

At a tumultuous open meeting, the citizens of New York turned down the merchants' pleas and voted to maintain the nonimportation policy. Conservative businessmen reacted by announcing they would take another poll.

McDougall and Isaac Sears, a fellow radical, decided to bring their own special kind of pressure into the fray and arranged for another mass meeting.[4] At first glance, it might have seemed natural for McDougall, considering his business interests, to go along with the other merchants. But by this time his concern for politics outstripped his personal economic motives. His group voted again for nonimportation and then marched down the streets, pausing at the doors of conservative merchants, who were loudly booed.

The conservatives, meanwhile, had rallied their own mob. The two groups, armed with clubs, converged on Wall Street. There, in the narrow lane faced on both sides by handsome brick houses and shops, the shouting, cursing bands battled for several hectic minutes until the pro-merchant forces gained the upper hand. Nursing black eyes and bloody noses, the radicals retreated. Their defeat was even more bitter to them when the second poll was completed—a vote for trade with London.

It was a low point for the radicals. Outraged Philadelphians charged that New York had "deserted the cause of liberty and your country." The Sons of Liberty in the Quaker City wrote to a chagrined McDougall and his colleagues to suggest that "the old Liberty Pole of New York should be transferred to that city as it no longer formed a rallying point for the votaries of freedom at home."[5] People in New Jersey and Connecticut, who normally carried on a heavy trade with New York, threatened to boycott the city. New York conservatives still were in control, as much because of disputes among the Whigs as their own strong leadership. The city and colony also were under intense pressures from Britain, much more so than many other colonies.[6]

The New York merchants were prepared for a certain amount of abuse for awhile but believed it would all blow over eventually. They soon had support for their action from the business interests of Philadelphia, who carefully contrived a meeting of sympathizers who voted for resumption of trade. At about the same time in other cities, patriotic fervor began to dim, replaced by demands for normal conditions and a reconciliation of differences with London.

McDougall and his friends were downhearted, frustrated by their defeats.[7] For awhile, they considered abandoning the fickle city, removing themselves to the supposedly free atmosphere of nearby Perth Amboy, New Jersey. There, they were convinced, they would find "easy navigation, delightful prospect, and healthful situation." They hoped such as move would ruin the Tory merchants of New York. Cooler heads, however, pointed out the difficulties and expense involved in such an operation, and the idea was dropped.

The pendulum seemed for a considerable time in the early 1770s to be swinging against the radicals. Many items again were imported from England, and some politicians on both sides of the Atlantic seemed convinced that outstanding differences would be worked out. Not much attention was paid to the noisy radicals who complained about curbs on the liberties of individuals. The colonies were mostly ignored in Parliamentary debate for many months.

It took a young British naval officer, Lieutenant William Dudington, to break the calm.[8] In March 1772, he sailed in an armed schooner, *Gaspee*, to the coast of Rhode Island where he was determined to end the ceaseless smuggling of contraband into that colony. Swooping down on the smugglers, who were accustomed to doing business without much interference, Dudington seized cargo after cargo. Even the pro-British merchants of Newport, who had been among the first to resume trade with Britain, were incensed. Most shippers and storekeepers throughout the colonies had long depended on non-British goods, much of which London considered contraband, for a substantial portion of their business.

The Rhode Islanders protested that Dudington was interfering with their personal rights. When his ship ran aground, they managed to attack and burn it. The British government was outraged by this open attack on its authority, and an official investigation was undertaken to determine who was responsible. The citizens of Rhode Island suddenly turned mute, unable to remember exactly who had taken part in the incident and how it had all begun. Powerless to make an example of anybody, the British washed their hands of the whole affair. It was a serious mistake. London's reluctance to pursue the matter later helped to persuade Boston patriots that they could get away with the same kind of behavior at the Boston Tea Party.

The Bostonians were upset by an attempt by Lord North, the British Prime Minister, to bail the East India Company out of its financial troubles in 1773 by giving it a monopoly in tea sales to the American colonies. The Tea Act, at the same time, reasserted Britain's right to tax the sales. McDougall and other radicals, only too pleased to have such an issue handed to them, hurried to their presses and ground out protest after protest against what they considered to be still another blow against American freedom.

Pro-radical editors urged a boycott of the tea, and sea captains were warned not to transport the product. The Sons of Liberty in New York reorganized to declare that they would "regard as enemies all those who took part in the tea business."

McDougall personally helped to persuade a considerable number of townspeople to boycott tea because of his ardent sympathy for the Bostonians. He complained, however, in a letter to the Boston

Committee of Correspondence that it had taken a great effort on the part of the patriots, and that the effort was "not without secret opposition."9 He added that "the worst that can happen here is the landing of the tea and storing it in the forts."

In New York, as elsewhere in the colonies, the Tea Act was debated extensively. Some newspapers called the law a grave attack on American liberties, but a number of influential citizens considered the matter of little importance.

McDougall and his allies found the act to be the spark they had been looking for during the three years of their eclipse. The Sons of Liberty again took to the streets, and, at a mass meeting in October, expressed their thanks to the captains who had refused to accept cargoes of tea from Britain. After another meeting the following month, tea agents in the city were persuaded not to sell any of the merchandise taxed by London. A band of "Indians" promised to use force against anybody who handled the product.

In late November, a revitalized "Association of the Sons of Liberty" took shape under the leadership of McDougall, John Lamb, and Isaac Sears. The group vowed that it would strike out against anybody who either bought or sold dutied tea.

For awhile, it looked as if there would be violence over the question of whether tea could even be landed and stored in the fort, as Governor Tryon wanted. McDougall and Sears gathered their forces to discuss the matter on December 17 at a mass meeting attended by 2,000 New Yorkers. Messages were read from Boston and Philadelphia announcing the decisions of those two cities to reject tea shipments, and the crowd voted to do the same, despite opposition by the mayor. In fact, no tea ship arrived until several months later, and by that time, it was academic that any vote had ever been taken.

The die was cast in Boston the night before the public meeting in New York—unknown at that time to the patriots of Manhattan. Three companies of fifty men, disguised as Indians, climbed aboard three ships in the Boston harbor and tossed overboard a large shipment of tea. It was a bold challenge to Parliament, which this time would have to pursue the matter to a conclusion.

When news of the Boston Tea Party reached New York, rushed on horseback by Paul Revere, the Sons of Liberty cheered their New England brethren and pledged to take similar action. True to

Tea and Bloodshed

their word, a tea shipment that finally arrived in New York was seized by "Indians" and thrown into the harbor.

The New York incident, however, was much more orderly than the Boston affair, and came to an almost comical end the following morning when the captains of the ships involved, who had been detained by the patriots, were politely escorted back to their vessels. As they were leaving the dock, a band struck up what seemed to some New Yorkers a curiously inappropriate tune: "God Save the King." It proved, however, that good manners were still important to some in New York.

In retaliation to what it considered American insolence, Parliament quickly passed the Boston Port Bill. The measure closed down the New England harbor to all shipping until the Bostonians paid for damages caused by the tea party. Many conservatives in the city were frightened, and advocated making amends. But the radicals, including the fiery Samuel Adams, were determined not to give in. They also asked for support from the other colonies, framing a "Solemn League and Covenant" which proposed that all Americans refrain from buying British goods or exporting to Britain until the Boston Port legislation was overturned. Paul Revere again raced on horseback to New York and Philadelphia to make the appeal.

On May 12, a ship arrived from England, officially informing New Yorkers the details of orders to close the Boston harbor. "This intelligence was received with great abhorrence and indignation by the Sons of Freedom," McDougall noted. "The officers of government endeavor to divide the people by intimating that nothing more was required by the Act than the payment for the tea, and that nothing was intended by Parliament against New York or any other of the colonies."[10]

Even the conservatives were angered by the Act, or at least professed to be.[11] McDougall observed that Oliver De Lancey had announced that he would rather spend every shilling of his fortune than comply with the legislation.

De Lancey's declaration, McDougall said, was merely "to amuse and dupe the Sons of Liberty to get their confidence in order that they may be more effectively deceived." McDougall, by this time, however, may have been so blinded by his dislike for De Lancey that he was unable to discern what may have been a genuine concern for the Bostonians.

Two days after the news arrived, McDougall noted that "Captain Sears spoke this day to a number of merchants to meet next Monday evening at Fraunces' Tavern in order also to determine on a nomination of a Committee of Correspondence to bring about a Congress."[12] McDougall and Sears were determined to encourage the boycott.

Most New York merchants, however, were afraid that a prolonged economic war with Britain would ruin business, and they stepped in to quiet the radicals. McDougall was pressured by his fellow merchants to use restraint. They suggested to him that "time will do everything for us if we maintain our firmness without violence."[13]

The businessmen also set about to cut the Sons of Liberty back to size. To reduce the influence of the radicals who controlled the group, the merchants and their friends packed the meetings to discuss the emergency.

McDougall noted on May 16: "To prevent a change of design or chicane in calling the meeting of the merchants, I had two advertisements wrote and put up this day at 11 A.M. of the Coffee House. . . . The Sons of Liberty, having no design in the meeting but to deliberate on the expediency of a nonimportation agreement and to get an impartial, spirited Committee of Correspondence appointed, used no acts to collect any person to the meeting."[14]

The De Lanceys, learning about the meeting, rounded up as many supporters as they could find. As a result, the gathering, overwhelmed by the conservatives, became so crowded that the group had to move out of Fraunces' Tavern into the larger Exchange Building. McDougall said the conservatives made it clear they intended to dominate from the moment they arose to speak.

"The majority of the company," McDougall said, "were for a committee of 15 or 21, but those who opposed the nominating a committee saw that it would be most favorable to their design to nominate a large committee. . . ."[15]

Led by the De Lanceys, the conservatives were influential in creating a Committee of Fifty, later expanded to Fifty-One. The merchants proceeded, McDougall said, to "pack" the committee by nominating their friends and omitting others known to favor the boycott.

A Mr. Janneys, McDougall complained, was put on the list of nominees "although I objected to him for his having told Samuel Broome 'that if the people of Boston opposed the landing the tea by force, they would be guilty of treason or rebellion. . . .'" Janneys denied he had said this, but McDougall didn't believe him.[16]

"In all Mr. Janneys' defense of this charge," the captain fumed, "he appeared in too much rage and confusion for an innocent man."

McDougall complained that "the whole of the business of this meeting, so far as the De Lanceys had any agency in it, evidenced a design to get such a committee nominated as would be under their direction with a view to gain credit with people if anything was done to advance the liberty cause—or to prevent anything being done, in which case they would make a merit of it with administration to procure places for themselves and their children."

The crowd was so surly that Isaac Sears was shouted down when he tried to read letters brought from Boston by Paul Revere.[17] The silversmith, according to McDougall, was carrying "a letter from Samuel Adams enclosing a vote of the Town of Boston, passed the 13th instant, and one from the Committee of Correspondence. These letters as well as the vote recommend a nonimportation and nonexportation of goods to Great Britain and the West Indies as the only effectual means to open their port and redress American grievances."

The tumult was so great that McDougall complained that "the enemies of our common liberties persist in their endeavors to divide the people and to lull them into a state of security."[18] He observed that "Ludlow the Marshal very impudently told me that 'he was opposed to a nonimportation and nonexportation agreement from interest, and that I should herd with those who were for it.'"

Although the election disappointed the radicals, they actually fared better than they had anticipated under the circumstances. Several radicals, including McDougall, were elected to the committee, and others turned out to be less conservative than the De Lanceys had guessed.

One member of the newly elected group, Gouverneur Morris, a member of a wealthy New York clan, said the meeting was a clear contest "about the future forms of our government, whether it should be founded upon aristocracy or democratic principles."[19]

He said the gathering was divided into two groups: the wealthy landlords and the tradesmen.

Morris observed, "The spirit of the English Constitution has yet a little influence left, and but a little. . . . The remains of it, however, will give the wealthy people a superiority this time, but would they secure it, they must banish all schoolmasters and confine all knowledge to themselves. This cannot be. The mob begin to think and to reason."[20] He concluded, "if the disputes with Great Britain continue, we shall be under the domination of a riotous mob."

The main problem facing the Committee of Fifty-One was to come up with a plan that would please the blood-thirsty radicals and not offend the conservatives who wanted to take no action at all. It was a real dilemma, and the group resolved it by embarking on a time-honored course favored by harried bureaucrats: proposing another committee to study the problem.

McDougall, a man of means who also was in touch with the lower classes, was a natural choice to help work out the details so the plan would win wide support. Laborers and tradesmen had been left out of many important political decisions in the recent past, and the radicals wanted to make sure it did not happen again. At the same time, nobody of substance wanted things to go too far so that the conservatives would be irreparably offended. Together with the committee chairman, Isaac Low, McDougall and two other prominent politicians, James Duane and John Jay, proposed a meeting of all the colonies to discuss America's growing problems at a Continental Congress. It was one of the earliest recommendations to hold such a gathering. In a letter to the Boston Committee of Correspondence dated May 23, 1774, the four New Yorkers wrote:

> The alarming measures of the British Parliament relative to your ancient and respectable town, which has so long been the seat of freedom, fills the inhabitants of this city with inexpressible concern; as a sister colony suffering in defense of the rights of America, we consider your injuries as a common cause. . . .[21]

The New Yorkers, however, observed that they could not offer any "decisive opinions" on their own about a remedy. All the colonies, they suggested, should be consulted about what to do. They declared:

Upon these reasons we conclude that a Congress of Deputies from the colonies in general is of the utmost moment; that it ought to be assembled without delay and some unanimous resolutions formed in this fatal emergency, not only respecting your deplorable circumstances, but for the security of our common rights. . . .

McDougall was on hand the next day when the history-making letter was handed to Paul Revere. "At 10 a.m.," the captain said, "Mr. Revere, the Boston express, departed for Boston with our letter to their committee. I urged upon him the expedience of their committee appointing time and place for the Congress as we did not do it in our letter."[22]

The Bostonians were upset by what they considered the inadequate response of New York, and replied that an intercolonial Congress, while desirable in the long run, would require too much time. Instead, they again urged a ban on trade with Britain.

The decision on whether to go all the way and support Boston's call for a boycott or back the New York recommendation for a Continental Congress fell to Philadelphia. There, as in New York, the moderates and conservatives wanted to avoid inflammatory action. The influential farmer-author, John Dickinson, advocated reasoning with the British, and appeared to oppose even a Congress. Under the circumstances, radicals such as Charles Thomson, known as the "Sam Adams of Philadelphia," feared they might be unable to persuade their fellow Pennsylvanians to support a meeting of all the colonies—much less a boycott. McDougall, hearing of the difficulties, wrote to Thomson that reports were being spread that Dickinson regarded the Boston Port Act as a constitutional law.

"This," McDougall complained, "is repugnant to the spirit of his former letters that in justice to him and the common cause of America I think he should be informed of it in order that if he is innocent (as I hope he is) he may contradict the calumny in the utmost speedy and effectual manner for his own honor and the advancement of the public liberty."[23]

Dickinson was so influential that Thomson and his friends decided that it would be unwise to confront him head on. Instead, they devised a scheme to bring him around without his realizing it. Capitalizing on Thomson's reputation as a firebrand, they arranged for the radical to speak first at a town meeting called to discuss the Boston controversy. He did so, delivering a fiery speech backing the Bostonians to the hilt. The conservatives booed and interrupted him constantly, and in the midst of his oration, he fainted—or at least pretended to collapse. As Thomson was carried from the meeting, Dickinson took over and addressed the throng on the need for moderation. Just as the radicals had hoped, he agreed with the New Yorkers that an all-colonies Congress was the best approach, and his advice was quickly accepted by a vote of the Philadelphians.

The call for a Congress was a triumph for the patriots, and the New Yorkers were especially exuberant. In a letter to Samuel Adams, McDougall and Isaac Sears declared:

> Lord North will find it to his great mortification that the Americans are not what he said they were: "a rope of sand." Be firm and a little time will effect your salvation and a glorious deliverance to America.[24]

Achievement and Disappointment 5

On a hot summer day in 1774, John Adams and fellow delegates from Massachusetts arrived in New York, en route to the First Continental Congress in Philadelphia. Although the meeting would not start until September, he wanted to consult with the New York activists with whom he had become friendly over the preceding, tempestuous months.

"Mr. McDougall and Mr. Platt came to see us," Adams wrote in his journal.[1] "Mr. Platt asked us to dinner next Monday. Mr. McDougall stayed longer and talked a good deal. He is a very sensible man, and an open one. He has none of the mean cunning which disgraces so many of my countrymen."

After dinner, McDougall and Platt accompanied Adams on a tour of the city. On the grounds of Fort George, overlooking the harbor, they inspected the ruins of the Governor's mansion. The once-imposing house had been destroyed by a fire of unknown origin six months previously. Governor Tryon and his family had made it to safety, but a sixteen-year-old servant girl, awakened from a sound sleep, had perished while trying to dress. About all that was salvaged from the ruins was the great seal of the province.

Adams and his friends then strolled through the remainder of the fort and through nearby Bowling Green which contained a gilded statue of King George III. Broadway impressed the Bostonian as "a fine street, very wide, and in a right line from one to the other end of the city." They passed churches, a college, a new hospital, a shipyard, markets, and a coffeehouse where they paused to read the newspapers. Adams was introduced to John Morin Scott, McDougall's lawyer at the libel trial, and the group proceeded to Hull's Tavern where they chatted until 11 P.M. McDougall's circle of friends and colleagues had grown considerably over the preceding months as even some semi-conservative New Yorkers, such as James Duane, became impatient with London's intransigence.

"McDougall was talkative, and appears to have a thorough knowledge of politics," Adams noted. "The two great families in this province, upon whose notion all their politics turn, are the De Lanceys and the Livingstons. There is virtue and abilities, as well as fortune, in the Livingstons, but not much of either of the three in the De Lanceys, according to him."

On Sunday, Adams went to the Old Presbyterian Society, which McDougall regularly attended, to hear a Dr. Rogers speak on the topic: "Seek first the Kingdom of God and His righteousness, and all other things shall be added unto you." McDougall then went to Adams' lodgings where they and Peter Livingston discussed the pro-British activities of the city's Church of England faction. They returned to the Presbyterian Church early in the afternoon for more preaching, which Adams liked, and singing, which he did not. Then they retired to McDougall's home, where they were joined by the New Hampshire delegates to the Congress. Adams found Mrs. McDougall to be "a charming woman" and the captain's daughter, Betsey, "an agreeable Miss."

Early the next morning, Adams and McDougall drove to breakfast with John Morin Scott at his manor house overlooking the Hudson River.[2] It was, Adams admitted, as elegant a breakfast as he had ever seen, with rich-looking silver tea service, an abundance of toast, "a plate of beautiful peaches, another of pears, and another of plums, and a muskmelon." The group advised the Bostonian to beware of Isaac Low, chairman of the Committee of Fifty-One, who "will profess his attachment to the cause of liberty, but his sincerity is doubted."

McDougall recommended that Adams avoid any reference in his conversations to "the last appeal"—revolution.

"He says," Adams wrote, "there is a powerful party here who are intimidated by fears of a civil war, and they have been induced to acquiesce by assurances that there was no danger, and that a peaceful cessation of commerce would effect relief. Another party, he says, are intimidated lest the leveling spirit of the New England colonies should propagate itself into New York." Adams also was told that another important group in New York was composed of merchants, like McDougall, dealing in the shipping trade, but, unlike McDougall, afraid of nonimportation because it might hurt their businesses. Another group was described as "those who are looking to the government for favors."

Later in the day, Adams was introduced to four New York delegates: James Duane, "between forty and forty-five," who watched the proceedings with a "sly, surveying eye, a little squint-eyed"; Philip Livingston, "a downright, straight-forward man"; John Alsop, "a soft, sweet man"; and Isaac Low.

Altogether, Adams spent a week in New York, and was wined and dined by all the Revolutionary leaders. He was, however, anything but overwhelmed by the hospitality, and concluded: "With all the opulence and splendor of this city, there is very little good breeding to be found. We have been treated with an assiduous respect, but I have not seen one real gentleman, one well-bred man since I came to town." Adams complained that New Yorkers "talk very loud, very fast and all together."

At last it was time for the Massachusetts delegates to leave for Philadelphia. McDougall was greatly disappointed that he was not making the same journey. He felt entitled to go, since he had been influential in raising the call for a Continental Congress. But in the tumultuous weeks preceding Adams' visit, McDougall had been battling with the New York conservatives, and, as usual, had lost. His opponents were particularly successful in delaying the initial attempts to assemble a Congress. The radicals, unable to break the conservative grip in the Committee of Fifty-One, called out their allies once more, and the streets were filled with shouting crowds who burned effigies of unpopular figures such as Lord North.[3] But the De Lancey group had seen it all before, and they remained steady.

McDougall and Sears wrote to Samuel Adams that it would take a push from Boston to get the Congress started. In the end, however, it was a chain of events in Philadelphia that made the difference.[4] A mass meeting in that city called for Pennsylvania's

Governor John Penn to assemble the legislature, but he would not do so. In mid-June, a group of Philadelphians, representing a cross section of classes, met to select a Committee of Forty-Three. Headed by John Dickinson, the group set up committees of correspondence throughout the province, and called for a Continental Congress.

In order to prevent any violence, Governor Penn reversed his decision and called the assembly into session. The conservative-dominated legislature then proceeded to elect seven delegates to the Congress, thus thwarting plans of the Committee of Forty-Three to pick its own slate.

The Sons of Liberty in other colonies were angered by Pennsylvania's action, and were determined not to let the same thing happen to them. At a June 29th meeting of New York's Committee of Fifty-One, McDougall proposed that the group nominate five deputies for Congress.[5] To assure that all voices were heard, he added that the list should be submitted to the Committee of Mechanics, mainly composed of lower-class workers. The conservatives countered with a suggestion that the delegates be elected by the legislature, as Pennsylvania had done. The radicals, naturally, opposed the idea, knowing that the assembly would pick a conservative slate.

When the committee met again on July 4, Sears proposed a list of five delegates, including McDougall, who were known to favor strong action against Britain.[6] The conservatives, however, had come to the meeting well prepared, and James De Lancey suggested an overwhelmingly moderate group which Adams later was to meet: Livingston, Alsop, Low, Duane and Jay. It was this slate the committee ultimately recommended to the public.

The radicals, who had been outmaneuvered, were incensed. They tried to recover by calling their supporters to an open meeting. On July 5, this handbill was posted across the city:

> The enemies of the liberty of America, being unwearied in misrepresenting the attachment of the inhabitants of this city to the common cause of this country, think it highly necessary to convene the good people of this metropolis in the Fields on Wednesday next . . . where every friend to the true interest of this distressed country is earnestly requested to attend—when matters

of the utmost importance to their reputation and security, as freemen, will be communicated.[7]

The workers showed up in great numbers on July 6.[8] Standing near the late afternoon shadow of the Liberty Pole, McDougall presided over a series of motions which included a strong pledge against importing British goods. McDougall denounced "the dangerous tendency of the numerous vile arts used by the enemies of America to divide and distress her councils, as well as the misrepresentations of the virtuous intentions of the citizens of this metropolis. . . ."

The crowd also was informed that the Committee of Mechanics had picked its own list of five delegates to Congress. The gathering accepted three of the five candidates on the Committee of Fifty-One slate, but substituted McDougall and Leonard Lispenard for James Duane and John Alsop.

Near the end of the meeting, a young man who had been pacing back and forth as the speeches continued, asked for and received recognition to address the crowd. Alexander Hamilton, a seventeen-year-old student at King's College, only recently arrived from the West Indies, began to speak hesitantly, among jeers about his boyish appearance. But he was equal to the test, and his voice grew stronger as he launched into a discussion of points he thought had been neglected. America, he said, should be united in resisting unconstitutional taxes and in backing "our brethren" in Boston. Refusal to import British goods, Hamilton argued, "will prove the salvation of North America and her liberties."

The crowd was pleased by Hamilton's remarks. The speech impressed McDougall, who, despite their age difference, immediately befriended the young man. They counseled together frequently, and McDougall loaned Hamilton many books from his library not only dealing with revolutionary matters but such subjects as philosophy and Latin as well.[9] The two were to maintain a close relationship until McDougall's death.

The selection of two rival slates in the city set off a heated campaign between the conservatives and radicals. The De Lancey group, believing its list was stronger, persuaded the Committee of Fifty-One to rule that voters must choose one or the other complete slate rather than individuals from either or both groups.

McDougall came to the reluctant conclusion that he must withdraw from the race so the city would not be wracked by division at a critical time. His opponents, however, claimed that McDougall saw the handwriting on the wall, and wanted to avoid the disgrace of defeat.

In a broadside to "the Freeholders, Freemen, and Inhabitants of the City and County of New York," McDougall wrote on July 9 that "when I consider the manner in which the Committee of Correspondence have determined to carry the resolutions at the City Hall into execution, I conceive your votes cannot be properly taken, and consequently the sense of the inhabitants will not be known."[10]

McDougall maintained that the public had expected to be able to vote for any five of the seven men nominated by the two factions, and that the Committee of Fifty-One's ruling to submit two complete slates instead "is unfriendly to liberty." Many New Yorkers, the captain declared, will refrain from voting if they cannot select the individuals they want.

"For these reasons and to end a contest which at present may be injurious to us," he explained, "I cannot think of putting you to the trouble of an uncertain poll without answering any valuable end, and, therefore, I decline the nomination of a deputy."

Thus, McDougall was not in Philadelphia for the convening of the Congress. The Sons of Liberty both in New York and Pennsylvania were downcast about their defeat by the conservatives. But they had achieved far more than they at first realized. They had prodded the reluctant hierarchy of those two provinces into helping form a Congress and sending delegations to the meeting. The mere presence of delegates from all areas gave the meeting a legitimacy it would otherwise have lacked.[11]

Furthermore, the Congress turned out to be far more receptive to "democratic ideals" than most people had anticipated. The conservatives arrived in Philadelphia prepared for sharp conflict with the New Englanders, who had been billed in advance as sharp-tongued and gross. Instead, the Yankees' calmness and gentlemanliness confounded the Tories. It was, to the surprise of many, the patrician southern planters, some educated in the best schools of England, who proved to be among the most vociferous against London. One Pennsylvanian commented, "There are some fine fellows come from Virginia, but they are very high. The Bostonians are mere milksops to them."[12]

Except for Georgia, all the colonies were represented in Congress. The first major item adopted was the Suffolk Resolves, originally approved by Suffolk County, Massachusetts. The resolutions rejected Britain's Coercive Acts as unconstitutional, recommended that Massachusetts form a government to collect taxes and keep them for the Crown, advised Americans to arm themselves, and proposed economic sanctions against London.[13]

Passage of the measure was a significant victory for the radicals in Congress, such as John and Samuel Adams and Patrick Henry. Conservative delegates tried to recoup by proposing a form of limited self-government for America while retaining strong ties with Britain. This union, however, was rejected—a further indication that Congress was headed for an irreversible split with London.

Underlining their strong feelings, the delegates then voted to halt trade with Britain. These were acts clearly unacceptable to the King and Parliament, and even the moderates who had hoped to reforge old links with the Mother Country realized that it might be impossible to prevent a war.

In New York, McDougall was working harder than ever to promote the patriots' cause on a continental basis, along lines laid down by Congress. Exchanging letters with the Committees of Correspondence in other colonies, he propagandized vigorously, further antagonizing his enemies. He had reason, he said, to suspect that he was under surveillance, complaining to Samuel Adams that his "letters to me have been intercepted. I must therefore request your favors be under cover to Mr. John Broome of this city, merchant."

McDougall insisted he had scrupulously conducted his own business to avoid dealing in British goods. Regarding the boycott, the captain commented that "I have had no small agency in these measures. I promoted them purely to maintain the union, to advance the safety of your people and the common cause." He observed to Adams that "whether I have been right in them, I must leave you and other friends to determine. Certain I am, what I did was in the integrity of my heart, for I have not imported any goods this two year."[14]

Faced with a hardening line throughout the colonies, even the conservative leadership of New York at last felt compelled to make some concessions. Their position had deteriorated as the Whigs resolved their differences and the storm of republicanism grew irresistible. Moreover, the Tory coalition of landholders, professionals and a smattering of small merchants and tradesmen was beginning to break apart. Time was on the side of the Whigs, whose membership ran from a few landed gentry to farmers, small businessmen, and laborers.[15]

In November, a somewhat more radical Committee of Sixty was elected to replace the Committee of Fifty-One.[16] The new group, which included McDougall and a larger group of his allies, gradually assumed more and more power while carrying out enforcement of the boycott. The former official bodies of government were steadily losing their authority.

McDougall was nominated in March 1775 as deputy to Congress in its second session.[17] Shortly before the election, however, he was involved in a demonstration that alarmed many moderates. The New York Sons of Liberty called a meeting at the Liberty Pole to discuss measures against the owner of a hardware store who had been accused of breaking the boycott. McDougall advocated not taking arms against the man or injuring him, and the crowd eventually broke up. The business interests, however, remembered only that McDougall had been part of the mob. They voiced their continuing doubts about him when the Provincial Congress met on April 21 to choose the delegation. McDougall was defeated, and another moderate slate was named. The euphoria of the victorious merchants, however, was not to last long. The day after the convention adjourned, Paul Revere rode into New York with news of the Battle of Lexington.

On the night of April 18, New Yorkers were told, redcoats had marched out of Boston in an attempt to destroy munitions stored at Concord.[18] The British hoped to surprise the patriots—and perhaps capture the rabble-rousers, John Hancock and Sam Adams as well—but Paul Revere and other riders spread the alarm from horseback.

Reports of the battles that ensued at Lexington and Concord stirred not only the colonies but also London and other capitals. The American patriots freely embroidered the incident to make it appear that the redcoats were murderers and savages, and that the battle had been planned as part of a campaign to rid the country of dissenting voices.[19]

It was becoming clear to many Americans that there would be no turning back, and the New York conservatives were further weakened. The city government, for the most part, was no longer functioning, so the Committee of Sixty emerged into a Committee of One Hundred to step into the breach. Preparations were made for hostilities. Steps ranged from an inventory of arms to a ban on shipping to the British-held ports of Boston and Halifax.

The New England delegation to the second Congress in Philadelphia discovered a much different mood in the city from the peaceful circumstances of the previous summer.[20] A crowd gathered to welcome the members and companies of citizens bearing muskets marched out seven miles to escort the group into the city amidst "shouts, noise, hurrahing, and riot." Isaac Sears, John Jay, and McDougall were among the leaders who greeted the New Englanders, including John and Samuel Adams and John Hancock. John Adams noted that the city "which had swayed so strongly one way in the autumn now swayed with equal impetus to the other side."

On May 22, New York organized its first Provincial Congress in which the patriots, including McDougall, were strongly represented.[21] One of the captain's first votes was against a measure backed by Gouverneur Morris to try to conciliate with London. Morris's plan was to concede Parliament's right to control trade, but to claim for the province the right to grant money to the British Treasury. The measure was approved by the congress, but it soon became a moot point as war preparations continued. Such activity, in fact, involved so many members that it became difficult to obtain a quorum. In July, the lawmakers conceded that they could no longer continue, and assigned many of their powers to a twelve-man Committee of Safety. The action was widely regarded as the province's real entry into the revolutionary movement. McDougall was a member of the select group, having finally won admission to the inner circle of power from which he had been excluded so long.

Invasion and Tragedy 6

New York was boiling with revolutionary fever in 1775. To some residents, it seemed as if war would break out there at any moment.

As a sample of what was to come, a crowd of hostile New Yorkers halted a British military column marching to the docks as the soldiers were preparing to embark for Boston.[1] The crowd let the soldiers pass, but forced them to abandon their carts filled with armaments. In the uproar, a soldier defected to the American side, and the troops, to the amazement of many, retreated without risking further trouble. It was a time of great anguish for hundreds of residents who were still loyal to Britain. Many of them were imprisoned and harassed.

In Philadelphia, Congress appointed George Washington as commander-in-chief of the American forces, and preparations were made to lay siege to the British army in Boston.

In New York, the revolutionaries had seized most of the reins of government through their committees. There was only a semblance of British rule left. The royal governor, William Tryon, with little but his title left intact, eventually would be forced to virtual exile aboard a ship in the harbor. But, at least for a brief period in June, he still had some prestige left when he returned to the city after a long visit to England.[2] He was entitled to a ceremonial welcome upon his return, but his arrival coincided, by chance, with the visit of the new commander-in-chief on his way to Massachusetts. The citizens resolved the dilemma of whom to welcome by arranging an official reception for each, at separate times and places, of course.

General Washington arrived first by boat from New Jersey. Accompanied by soldiers, local patriot politicians, and exuberant townspeople, the tall Virginian was escorted to Hull's Tavern, an elegant hotel favored by the Sons of Liberty. He would not remain long, however. Word came on that very day that the Americans had lost an important battle at Breed's (Bunker) Hill. It was high time, obviously, for him to step into the breach in Massachusetts.

Several hours after Washington's arrival, Tryon landed and was greeted by a smaller, pro-loyalist party. A competent, intelligent soldier-administrator, he had won over not only the conservatives but also some of the middle-of-the-roaders by remaining sympathetic to colonial problems while carrying out some policies he personally disliked. Tryon also had won a grudging respect from some patriots by announcing, when he first became governor some years before, that he, not the De Lanceys, would head the province. The governor was escorted by his friends past Fraunces' Tavern, along the wide and handsome expanse of Broad Street to a town house on Broadway where he would temporarily reside. The Governor's mansion, as John Adams had noted during his stroll with McDougall, had been destroyed by fire previously.

By now, most authority was in the hands of the new Provincial Congress, which was meeting at City Hall. The item of highest priority before Congress was to raise the army expected of them and every other colony.

In the coffee houses and taverns, arguments abounded over Thomas Paine's pamphlet *Common Sense*.[3] In it, the young man openly dared to argue in favor of war and independence—a far cry from the comparatively mild message that had landed McDougall in so much trouble.

"Everything that is right or natural pleads for separation" (from Britain), Paine declared. "The blood of the slain, the weeping voice of nature cries 'TIS TIME TO PART.'"

A group of conservative New Yorkers wrote their reply to the pamphlet and announced they would publish it.[4] Before the reply could be distributed, however, the radicals, nursing old grudges against the conservatives, decided to give them a dose of their own medicine. John Lamb, Isaac Sears, and McDougall met at a dockside tavern and agreed to take forceful steps against the conservatives' printer, Mr. Loudon. McDougall evidently had no qualms about the matter, managing to ignore his previous defense of the freedom of the press when he was in the minority.

At midnight, they and several friends broke into Loudon's house, hauled him out of bed, and destroyed the pamphlets as well as the form on which they had been printed. To avoid being outflanked, they also sent every other printer in the city a note which read: "Sir, if you print or suffer to be printed in your press anything against the rights and liberties of America or in favor of our inveterate foes, the King, Ministry and Parliament of Great Britain, death and destruction, ruin and perdition shall be your position. Signed, by order of the committee of tarring and feathering, LEGION."

The radicals retaliated even more violently against James Rivington, publisher of the pro-Tory *Rivington's New York Gazetteer*.[5] A lively and attractively printed weekly, the newspaper had aroused the wrath of the Sons of Liberty because of its slanted coverage of the boycott and a long series of insults to radical leaders. Typically, the *Gazetteer* had called Isaac Sears "the laughing stock of the whole town," and the newspaper's columns repeatedly underplayed support for the boycott and overemphasized the conservative side.

Critics said Jemmy Rivington, who had emigrated from England some years before, was merely playing up to the social aristocracy of the city, upon whom he was dependent for advertising and private printing contracts. A fat, well-dressed, intelligent man, he loved to hobnob with the wealthy at their parties where he was an entertaining companion. For a few months after a mob had nearly wrecked his business, he "reformed" and printed news more favorable to the radicals. But he eventually returned to his old style, and negative comments about the boycott again prevailed in his columns.

Rivington thus was a natural target for Captain Sears and a band of vigilantes who stormed into New York after rallying in Connecticut. They were determined to harass their enemies. After "arresting" and abusing several prominent citizens, they broke into Rivington's shop and systematically destroyed his type—imported at great cost from England—and smashed his presses. Cheered on by a crowd of spectators, they completed their job without interference from any authorities. Rivington, fearing for his life, fled to a British warship in the harbor. In later years, he may have had a change of heart, for there are indications he aided the American cause during the Revolution, posing all the while as pro-British.

McDougall was accused of having taken part in the raid. He obviously resented the accusation and sought official verification that he had not been involved. In a document McDougall acquired some years later, Lewis Morris, who became a general in the American army, wrote that he had encountered McDougall and John Jay one evening in 1775 at Jay's home. Lewis was told that a mob was forming to attack Rivington's house.

"Mr. Jay expressed his aversion to such a measure," Morris recalled, "and requested me to step to the place of meeting and prevent such their intention from being executed. General McDougall was of the same sentiments with Mr. Jay and strongly expressed his abhorrence of such a measure, at the same time requesting me to urge the people that Rivington was not long since a bankrupt and that he had no doubt his house was mortgaged for its full value, so that the loss by such destruction would not fall upon Rivington but upon some other person who might be one of our friends, which I accordingly did."[6]

Despite such disorders, New Yorkers generally were less militant than many other Americans, especially New Englanders. The reasons for New York's conservatism are still being debated, but at least one factor was the enormous power and respect which wealthy landholders commanded right up to the Revolution. Writing to a Boston patriot, McDougall complained that "Sure I am, we shall be the last of the provinces to the northward of Georgia that will appeal to the sword."[7] Warning his Massachusetts colleague about New York's passive nature, McDougall said "your ignorance of this might lead you into measures which might be fatal to yourselves and to all America. We have not yet chosen delegates to meet the next Congress. . . ."

One of the most important tasks confronting the New York radicals was how to enforce the boycott. They did so by threatening New York merchants with economic ruin and violence, including death, if they imported British goods. To guard against violations by businessmen attempting to smuggle merchandise into the city, the militants set up small harbor patrols to monitor ships suspected of carrying merchant cargo from London.

McDougall frequently reported on these activities to Josiah Quincy, a prominent Massachusetts lawyer who had traveled to London to enlist help for the American cause.[8] The captain noted a steady improvement of the New York radicals, and cited as an example the case of a London-bound vessel, *Beulah,* which had been prevented from landing in New York.

The owners, Robert and John Murray, took the opportunity of a stormy night to land their goods. When they were accused by a patriot committee, they confessed.

McDougall observed: "Our citizens were so enraged at them for the horrid deed that it was with great difficulty that they were prevailed upon not to banish them." McDougall also noted that "this is the only violation of the Association we have had since it took place. The punishment they now and will endure is sufficient to deter any man, however brave, from another breach. The friends of the Association and the great cause are daily increasing so that you have no reason to fear a defection of this colony."

In May, the last hopes of the conservatives in New York and the other colonies for a peaceful settlement with Britain were laid to rest. Congress, incensed by British action at Lexington, voted that "these colonies be immediately put into a state of defense." Provision was made for an American army of 20,000 men, with George Washington as commander-in-chief.

It was clear from the start that New York would eventually become a major battleground, and General Washington, during his brief stopover in the city, had taken time to consider the area's defenses, or lack of them. Accompanying him were two other recently appointed generals, Charles Lee and Philip Schuyler. General Schuyler, a wealthy revolutionary from Albany, had been named commander of the Continental army in the province. He was a veteran of the French and Indian War, had served in the New York militia for many years, and was one of the region's few officers experienced in warfare. But despite his family connections with every leading clan in the province, he was unable to persuade other members of the gentry to take the initiative in gearing for hostilities. For awhile, it looked as if it would be extraordinarily difficult, if not impossible, to find the men to fill the four regiments requested of New York.

The province had been asked to supply more than 3,000 men—ten companies of seventy-seven officers and enlisted men in each regiment.[9] Each company was to be led by a captain and four lieutenants. All such units also had three sergeants, three corporals, and a fifer and a drummer.

One of the first to undertake the task of recruiting the First New York Regiment was Alexander McDougall—fired by revolutionary fervor and ambitious for military rank. With little or no funding from provincial coffers, he threw himself into the effort with enthusiasm, often paying bills with his own money. Many of his recruits, like himself, were ex-sailors, and the majority were poor and unlettered.

They came in large part from the Out Ward, an area to the north of the main part of the city. The neighborhood included some of the port's worst slums as well as farms beyond the residential and commercial streets. There were few bluebloods and virtually none with military experience, particularly in the rough skills needed for camping and marching in the province's vast forests, but they were eager and willing. Each day, they paraded on the commons in front of their barracks and were drilled in military techniques.

In recognition of his efforts, McDougall was appointed a colonel to head his regiment. One of his first assignments was on orders from General Schuyler: to fortify the city against attack. Except for a few cannon, New York was virtually defenseless, and McDougall knew there was little time to set up substantial armaments.

For some time, a number of prominent New Yorkers had had their eyes on the naval cannon left behind by the British at Fort George—the property and responsibility of the Crown. Some American officers suggested that the guns be removed before the British could reclaim them, and that they be transferred to the American forts being planned to guard the highlands. A decision was made to go ahead with the work if the cannon could be pulled out without alarming the British aboard the warship, *Asia*.

Late one night, a group of soldiers converged on the battery and began dismantling the twenty-one guns, each of which weighed more than a ton.[10] The men slowly began to drag the huge weapons away from the waterfront. Lieutenant Alexander Hamilton was part of the force stationed at the water's edge to guard against a British attack, but when there was no sign of alarm even from a nearby small boat filled with British sailors, he decided he would be of more help assisting with the guns.

In the dead of night, when the work was still under way, a sailor in the sloop fired a shot, perhaps as a signal to *Asia*. The nervous Americans on shore opened fire on the small boat, killing one of the sailors. The *Asia* crew opened fire with its cannon, mainly as a warning, and the city awakened to its first sound of war. Some householders ran into the streets in panic, while others hid in their basements. A substantial number headed for the woods beyond the city. Another round of fire from *Asia* missed Fort George, but damaged a number of nearby buildings. Governor Tryon, who had been with friends on Long Island, hurried back to the port to try to stop the violence. The thoroughly shaken New Yorkers were willing to listen, and agreed to compromise. The cannon were left at the point to which they had been dragged (on the Commons), but the Americans promised not to move them any farther. The incident ended without additional bloodshed, yet it was evident that nothing really had been settled.

The presence of powerful British naval forces under the noses of the New Yorkers also served as a reminder to many Americans that they should lose no time building their own fleet. McDougall, commenting on the situation to John Jay, warned that the American fleet—which, at the start, would be much smaller than the British force—should operate defensively.[11] It would be folly, McDougall said, to attempt a major engagement against the enemy "where there is danger of the force being near equal before your officers and men are practiced in sea engagements. If it is, our American fleet, I fear, will not be long in our possession. I know that so much depends on address and preparation founded on experience that I tremble for the consequences. A small omission determines the fate of a sea engagement. I speak with confidence, because it is from experience. It has been the business of my life."

The problems of setting the mobilization in motion were staggering, and McDougall, despite his enthusiasm, more than once became frustrated and angry. "I have used the utmost diligence in and out of Congress to appoint and complete the regiments under my command," he told General Schuyler. "But my utmost efforts have not enabled me to appoint more than four companies, which were embarked yesterday under the command of Colonel [Rudolphus] Ritzema with a fair wind for Albany."[12]

Ritzema, the son of a Dutch Reformed clergyman and former officer in the British Army, was McDougall's second-in-command. Another contingent was led by Lieutenant Colonel William Goforth, a lawyer and veteran radical.

McDougall complained of a "want of money and clothes" for the effort, and said it had been exceedingly difficult to collect the rifles that a mob had seized from the city armory. The officer noted bitterly that when the arms were sent for repair to the gunsmiths, "for want of money to discharge their bills, they gave the preference to other work."

To John Jay, who later became the first Chief Justice of the United States, he commented that "the Tories are cheerful, and too many of the Whigs make long faces. Men of rank and consideration refuse to accept of commission as field officers of the militia, so that these commissions have gone abegging for six or seven weeks."[13] This particular complaint got quick results. Jay applied to McDougall for a commission, and was named a colonel of the New York militia.

Supplies also were a problem, and McDougall wrote to friends in Philadelphia to prevail upon Congress for more gunpowder for the colony. "We have not 300 pounds [of gunpowder] at our command if it would save the colony," the officer warned, "and the inhabitants are very illy supplied—not a quarter of a pound per man in the hands of half the citizens, and the country much worse. This is a deplorable state to be in for men who have their all at stake. For God's sake, quicken the replacing of our powder."

Although the attention of most Americans was fixed on Boston, where General Washington's forces faced some of Britain's best battle-hardened veterans, a move was under way to undertake an offensive on another front: Canada. Frontiersman Ethan Allen and Colonel Benedict Arnold had captured small British forts at Crown Point and Ticonderoga, far north of New York City, and Congress was elated. The lawmakers believed that it would not be difficult to follow up those victories with an invasion of Canada, which would be sealed off as a possible launching point for a British attack on the rebellious colonies.

A substantial part of McDougall's troops were sent north in August to join the forces rallying for the invasion. The officer himself remained in the city, attempting to complete the recruitments and supervise the building of new fortifications. Some criticized McDougall for staying behind, but many fellow officers, who understood the problems involved, approved his decision.

Standing in for him in the invasion forces were his sons, John and Ranald Stephen. Under the command of General Schuyler and Brigadier Richard Montgomery, they moved northward in the fall of 1775. On September 5, they reached a small stronghold, Fort St. Johns, near what is now the New York-Quebec border, where they were stalled by a disciplined British contingent. For nearly two months, the British held out against an American siege—effectively delaying the planned assault on Montreal until the bitter winter had set in. Eating reduced rations and camping out in increasingly cold and rainy weather, the Americans grew steadily more discouraged and ill.

Colonel William Goforth wrote from the encampment that McDougall's son, John, "is looked upon to be a brave soldier. Your son, Stephen, recovered from his illness I acquainted you of before, and has since been quite hearty, but yesterday, leaving the quarter yard and being very wet, he this morning finds himself very poorly. . . . A little rest and dry weather, I hope, will cure him."[14]

In late October, McDougall relayed to John Jay the news that his troops in Canada "were healthier than they had been" and were in good spirits, well supplied with fresh provisions. He noted that "one of our bombs had fired a large house, the principal barrack in the [British] fort, but was extinguished. . . . From all I have been able to collect, the fort is completely invested and so near that the besiegers can hear the garrison speak to each other." McDougall

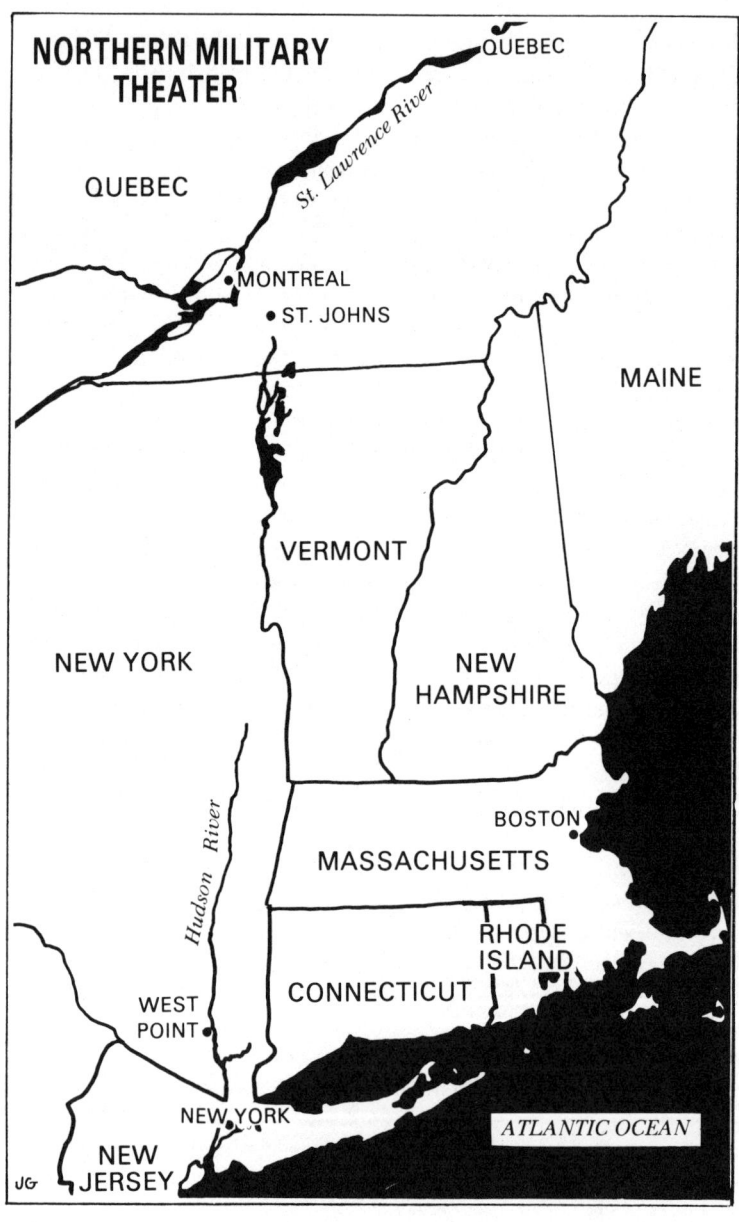

Invasion and Tragedy

deplored the fact that the Americans "are not strong enough to make any sallies," and concluded that "if we do not succeed, it will be for want of engineers and ammunition."

After fifty-five days of resistance, Fort St. Johns surrendered, and the Americans moved on toward Montreal. They crossed the St. Lawrence River on November 12 and seized the town. The American soldiers were jubilant, but, for Colonel McDougall, the joy was not to last long. A few days later, he received this letter from Colonel Ritzema in Montreal: "Your son, poor Jack, is no more. He died this day . . . at Laprairie [near Montreal] after a few days illness of a bilious fever."[15] Young McDougall was buried with military honors in the cemetery of a graystone church which towered above the flat plain, visible for miles around. The village priest was persuaded only with the greatest difficulty to allow the burial of a Protestant youth—whose name was never recorded in the church registry. Colonel McDougall in New York was heartbroken, but persevered with his recruiting and training programs.

Ritzema also informed McDougall that "the General is now remodeling the Army—he is sending the lame, the blind, the halt, the lazy and the lads who are homesick and of too delicate a texture to encounter more hardships and this frigid clime to their mammies and daddies and wives and pumpkin pies."

Another officer complained to McDougall that "we have been most shamefully neglected. I know not where the fault lies, but we have neither money nor credit, nor a third of troops we ought have."[16]

General Montgomery, well aware of the severity of the Canadian winter, had intended to remain in Montreal for the rest of the season. He learned, however, that Benedict Arnold had led a small force through the woods of Maine to the St. Lawrence near Quebec. Montgomery made plans immediately to join him for an attack on Quebec—known to be much better defended than Montreal. Leaving most of his men behind, he hurried down the river by boat to confer with Arnold. McDougall was notified in a dispatch from Montreal on November 22 that "Colonel Arnold is before Quebec with 800 men. We expect in a few days, perhaps tomorrow, to move toward that place. . . . Your son, Stephen, is very hearty."

The youth was described as "a good lad, behaves well and with as much prudence and sobriety as must be expected from a young man."[17]

Colonel McDougall was worried, and he confided to Jay in Philadelphia that he was "anxious to hear what is determined in your cabinet with respect to Canada for the next campaign. Colonel Ritzema and Colonel Goforth both write me from Montreal that 10,000 men will be necessary to secure the colony and engage the Canadians heartily in the cause."[18]

Before such plans could be realized, however, the invasion was to come to a climax on quite a different note. As a blizzard descended on the city of Quebec on the night of December 30, the Americans prepared to attack, hoping to capture the fortress before its defenders could rally. But a deserter had informed the British commander, General Guy Carleton, of the American scheme, and he alerted his men. General Montgomery, leading his troops through the blinding snow, was killed in one of the first charges, and Arnold was wounded in the leg. A Virginia rifleman, Daniel Morgan, led his own soldiers past a frightened group of New Englanders and tried without success to rally them for a further assault. The British soldiers were terrified of the riflemen, who were whooping like Indians, but strong British defensive positions and American confusion eventually ended in defeat for the colonials. Morgan was among about 400 prisoners taken.

It was essentially the end of the invasion, although the Americans maintained their siege for several months longer. Lieutenant Ranald Stephen McDougall was among the remaining force outside the city walls—an assignment he had chosen despite the advice of other officers to stay in Montreal. Colonel Goforth explained in a letter to the young man's father that the youth had been ill for some time, and was "much distressed that his state of health would not permit him to go."[19] At first, Lieutenant McDougall took "Dada [Daddy] Goforth's advice, saying he knew his father would be satisfied if he was advised by him." At length, however, the young officer said he was feeling better, and persuaded his commander that he should be allowed to proceed to Quebec.

When warm weather returned, the British, as expected, arrived in a large fleet with reinforcements from London. Sailing steadily

Invasion and Tragedy

upriver, the British easily overpowered a small group of tiny American vessels, which included the schooner, *Mary*. Its twenty-four-man crew, fearing for their lives, fled to the shore, leaving behind one officer—Lieutenant McDougall. A fellow prisoner, noting the youth's capture in his diary, commented: "By the news he brings we are in hopes things are not so bad as the people of the garrison reported. However, I think it is bad enough."[20]

The remaining American forces, who came to the same conclusion, limped slowly home. Colonel McDougall complained to Jay that "the northern expedition cost me my eldest son, and the other, Ranald McDougall, was made a prisoner in Canada."[21] The New Yorker asked Jay to use his influence in Congress, which was preparing lists of prisoners for exchange with the British, to make sure his son was not forgotten. "The sooner you do it, the more you will oblige me," the colonel noted.

Ranald McDougall was eventually exchanged, and rejoined his father's command, but he never fully regained his health. The fruitless Canadian campaign had exacted a bitter personal price of Colonel McDougall and his family.

The Army Is Saved 7

*I*n the early months of 1776, New York—as yet unscarred by full-scale war—nevertheless was beginning to look like a city under siege. Long trenches were being dug, breastworks erected, and cannon put into place against the possibility of a naval attack.

Hundreds of residents, both loyalists and patriots, had left the city and fled with their most precious possessions to the comparatively safe rural areas of New York, Connecticut, and New Jersey. Others boarded boats for Canada and the West Indies. Many of the province's most prominent citizens, such as Myles Cooper, president of King's College, and James De Lancey, escaped to England to avoid the wrath of the patriot mobs.[1] By late spring, the majority of the city's civilian populace was gone, their houses locked and shuttered. Soldiers were everywhere, and, in the midst of it all, Alexander McDougall was trying to outfit new recruits, feed and house his own men and those from neighboring areas, help select and supervise the construction of defense works, and assist in running the city government.

It was a maddening combination of duties, but, despite everything, the defenses were beginning to take shape. In mid-March, McDougall received an urgent request from General Washington.[2] The commander's aide, writing from Cambridge, informed McDougall that Washington would be proceeding to New York, and wanted "the favor of your hiring for him a large house ready furnished somewhere in or about the Bowery Lane. His family is large and he has a number of horses. You will therefore see the necessity of a spacious house and large stables."

The location McDougall chose was a splendid mansion with a large lawn that stood at the top of Richmond Hill, overlooking the Hudson. It was cleaned and outfitted with a housekeeper, cook, and steward, who awaited the general's arrival.

In the meantime McDougall relayed to General Schuyler rumors of an impending attack on New York by the troops formerly based in Boston.[3] "Generals Washington and Greene," McDougall advised, "seem to be of the opinion they [the British] intend coming here."

McDougall complained that the city was badly prepared for the fight. "Our stock of provision is insufficient even for musketry," he observed, "and shall stand in great need of the use of cannon. The ground not broke on Long Island for the fortified camp. . . ."

The New Yorker also grumbled that if "my advice had been taken last summer, we should have had saltpeter and arms in no small quantities made in the colony. But it's the curse of our public affairs that a criminal parsimony and want of wisdom to anticipate events even the friends of our country cannot be brought to provide for contingencies."

Although there was considerable confusion among the Americans about the intentions of Britain's General William Howe, McDougall advised Schuyler on March 21 that "appearances were so strong in favor of total evacuation of the town [Boston] that the General [Washington] ordered six regiments to march to New York, and a body of riflemen, and expected soon to follow himself. . . ."[4]

For weeks, Washington had been concerned about the status of New York's defenses. The American army's able third-in-command, General Charles Lee, more or less took it upon himself to lead an expedition to the city to determine what had been done and what remained to be accomplished. The English-born officer, a short, ugly, irascible man who was one of America's few experienced warriors, was shocked at what he found.

For one thing, the royal governor, William Tryon, was still maintaining a semblance of British authority from an armed royal ship in the harbor. His powers were diminished, but his advice was sought by many of the remaining citizens. Another irritation was the continuing influence of a stubborn group of Tories, who abhorred revolution.

"You are, it seems, afraid of your town," Lee wrote. "In the first place, I do not believe that they [the British] dare fire upon it, but if it was earnestly their intention, you have, I think, the means of preventing it."[5]

Lee was aghast at what he considered Tryon's attempts to regain control of the colony by engineering the election of a pro-Tory slate to the Assembly. "What the devil business has Tryon or any other delegate of an accursed [British] Ministry to interfere at all in the affairs of America?" the general asked McDougall. "The Crown and Ministry are now in open actual war with the colonies. Any one colony, therefore, that at present acts by direction of the Crown or its delegates is guilty of high treason to the continent. I know not whether you view these things in the same heinous light with me, but at least you must allow that hobbling on one high-heeled shoe and one low one like the Prince of Lilliput gives you a mighty uncouth air."[6]

Lee apologized for expressing himself so bluntly, but added that "unless I mistake your turn of mind, I should offend more by reserve than the most licentious utterance of my sentiments."

McDougall listened to Lee's complaints politely, and continued to go about his business as best he could. Tryon remained safely in his shipboard office; on shore, the patriot Committee of Safety actually held most of the reins of power. It was a most difficult arrangement, and problem after problem frustrated their plans. Some of the patriots despaired that their cause would be lost because of their own mistakes. McDougall complained to John Jay that a ship dispatched to Spain to pick up gunpowder had failed to do so because all of that material had been earmarked for Britain. "To add to our distress," the officer observed, "we have lost Judge [James] Livingston's mill by the carelessness of two men who fired off their guns near some of the pans in which powder was placed to dry."[7]

There was also the worrisome matter of what to do with wounded veterans of the Canadian expedition, who were straggling home. "I have been under no small embarrassment," McDougall told General Schuyler, "for want of knowing what was due to the sick and discharged men who lately came down almost naked and without the means of supporting themselves. From a principle of humanity, a regard to the public service, and to prevent our enemies improving their distress against the country, I advised the Congress to give them provisions in the barracks till their captains came down or till it was known what payments had been made to them."[8]

The officer also was concerned about enlistments which had not fulfilled his expectations. He was encouraged, however, by John Jay who wrote from Philadelphia that "New York never stood better with Congress than now. Your alacrity in raising and arming your troops last summer is compared with the tediousness and slow moving of others."[9]

McDougall also helped to build an American navy. He warned the American command and Congress that a well-trained fleet is essential to defeating the British, and urged the creation of a powerful force as soon as possible. Taking direct action in his own colony, he paid £325 for the sloop, *Sally*, which was converted into an armed blockade runner.[10] A bill of sale to the Committee of Safety identified McDougall as part owner of the ship. On occasion, he may have felt an urge to return to the sea, but his army duties clearly ruled that out.

John Jay wrote him that "your fitting out an armed vessel on the colony account does you honor. I am at liberty to inform you that the Congress have passed a vote for privateering, by which I hope the losses of some of our friends will be repaired."[11]

Jay also commented that no single flag had been adopted by Congress for the Continental fleet. Most captains, he said, selected their colors on the basis of "their own fancies and inclinations. I remember to have seen a flag designed for one of them on which was extremely well painted a rattlesnake rearing his crest and shaking his rattles, with this motto: 'Don't tread on me.' But whether this device was generally adopted by the fleet, I am not able to say. I rather think it was not."[12]

Under the double strain of exhausting civil and military duties, McDougall was sensitive to criticism that he had failed his troops by remaining at home when they marched to Canada. Jay relayed to him rumors in Congress that McDougall's regiments were not half full, and that he had been supplying the *Asia*. By tales like these, Jay observed, McDougall's critics "pay their court to people who have more ostensible consequence than real honesty, and more cunning than wisdom."

McDougall blamed these rumors for the failure of Congress to promote him to general, even though others whom he considered no more than his equals had been so honored. He complained to General Schuyler about the promotion of William Alexander of New Jersey, whom Americans called "Lord Stirling" even though Britain refused to recognize his claim to a Scottish title.[13] McDougall conceded, however, that on the eve of a British attack, it was not time to argue about rank. "If the Congress had put the lowest sergeant in my regiment over me," he declared, "I am determined to serve this campaign."

Jay complimented McDougall for accepting Stirling's promotion without further protest. "The spirit you betray on this occasion becomes a soldier," the lawmaker asserted.[14]

In the midst of all his other concerns, McDougall also was forced by the nature of his offices to deal with the difficult General Lee. Many New Yorkers were upset by the fact that the general had begun his march without consulting the authorities of the colony. In an age when each province to some degree regarded itself as a sovereign nation, the breach of etiquette was serious. There was also the matter of trying to house 5,000 troops in a relatively small city that already was badly disarranged by war preparations.[15] Lee apparently had anticipated resistance to his housing needs, but McDougall and John Morin Scott, representing the Committee of Safety, said the city would do its best to meet the Army's needs.

Lee's fears that the Tories would be able to take over the colony by popular consent also proved groundless. At an open air election, New York county voters rejected the Tory candidates and selected John Jay, Philip Livingston, John Alsop, and McDougall to the colonial Assembly.[16] Before long, Lee was well impressed by the willingness of New Yorkers to further the war effort—including physical labor on the defense works. His endeavors in the city, however, were clouded by constant quarreling over such matters as how to deal with British sympathizers.

The extent of continuing trade with the British, for example, came to light when a small ship, *Polly and Nancy*, was wrecked on the New Jersey coast.[17] The cargo included a substantial amount of contraband (part of which was a shipment of Madeira addressed to General Howe) and passengers bound for London via Boston.

John Graham, one of the travelers who had been placed under guard by the Committee of Safety after the wreck, addressed a personal plea for leniency to Colonel McDougall, explaining: "As I only went passenger by permission of His Excellency (Governor Tryon) in order to get my son home to New York, [I] think it is cruel. My state of health at present is such that if I have not my enlargement soon, I must inevitably perish."[18] Graham was freed a few days later.

It was by no means the only case involving help for the British by the New York Tories.[19] A substantial number of harbor pilots were suspected of guiding incoming ships not to the city docks but to a British man-of-war, *Phoenix*, which had seized several vessels. Among them was McDougall's old ship, *Sally*. An informer pinpointed a secret camp out of which the Tory pilots were operating, but a patrol requested by McDougall found only an abandoned campsite. The pilots apparently had been forewarned, and had taken refuge aboard *Phoenix* to avoid revenge from the revolutionaries.

Unexpectedly, the long-awaited attack on New York was delayed for several months while the British concentrated on a southern campaign. Encouraged by royalist sentiment among many southerners, the redcoats headed by ship for the Carolinas, where they anticipated an easy victory. When they arrived off North Carolina, however, they discovered that a group of loyalist Scottish settlers had prematurely attacked an American force at Moore's Creek Bridge and had been soundly defeated. The patriots had jailed the Scottish leaders, and the Americans were in control of the colony.

General Henry Clinton, who wanted to salvage something of the campaign, turned his attention instead to the tempting, prosperous port of Charleston, South Carolina. The city, one of the largest in America, exported rice and other crops to Europe and the West Indies and imported manufactured goods. It also was one of the best defended communities in the South. On an island in the harbor, American forces were well entrenched in a fort which could not be bypassed if the city was to be taken from the sea.

The Army Is Saved

General Charles Lee, who had been rushed south to take command there—much to the relief of many New Yorkers—advised a subordinate, Colonel Moultrie, to abandon the island. Moultrie, luckily, refused, and stoutly resisted the British attack. The palmetto-log fort withstood a heavy twelve-hour bombardment, while the British fleet, on the other hand, suffered heavy losses from the American cannon. At last, the British withdrew and sailed north to reinforce the attack on New York.

General Washington was now personally in command on Manhattan Island. He was the toast of New York—applauded by all but the Tories for his forceful intelligence, diplomacy, and graceful Virginia manners. But the southerner also had powerful enemies in the city among the few and stubborn loyalists who had chosen to remain. Not long after Washington's return to New York, they began to plot to get rid of him and other leaders. The plan was discovered shortly before it was to have been executed, however, and some forty people were arrested. Among them were members of Washington's own corps of bodyguards, including Thomas Hickey, who allegedly had been designated to poison a serving of peas on the general's plate. Hickey was hanged, but the patriot leaders remained on their guard, fearful of other such plans.

Despite a diminished population and martial activity all around them, New York's remaining citizens went ahead with an election for the Provincial Congress. It produced one major surprise: defeat for Colonel McDougall. A large number of voters resented his decision not to accompany his troops to Canada and suffer alongside them. Many thought McDougall had taken the easy way out and deliberately avoided combat—even though that probably was not his intention, for he was not a man to shirk his duty. He believed he was right to have stayed behind, raising more troops and supplies. Nevertheless, he was deeply hurt, and confessed his anguish to friends.

John Jay, trying to console him, admitted the election had "taken a turn I did not expect."[20] Nonetheless, Jay added, "the zeal you have shown and the sacrifices you have made in this great cause will always afford you the most pleasing reflections and will one day not only merit but receive the gratitude of our fellow citizens. Posterity, you know, always does justice."

It was not long, however, before concern over such relatively minor affairs evaporated before the much more pressing urgencies of the war. The British launched their long-awaited attack on New York on July 2, and seized Staten Island without opposition. Day after day, ships arrived from London with arms, equipment, and men. It was a disheartening sight for the Americans across the harbor on Manhattan and Long Island, but they bravely proclaimed independence on July 18—severing forever their familial ties with England. As if to emphasize their decision, a group gathered on Bowling Green and pulled down the statue of King George. There was no cheering, only an eerie calm. The broken image was further ripped with crowbars; eventually its lead would be used to make bullets for the Americans.

Washington was uncertain where the British would concentrate their main attack, so he divided his forces (totaling about 20,000 men) between Manhattan and Long Island.[21] General Howe, on the other hand, had approximately 30,000 redcoats and the advantage of surprise. On August 22, he moved the first of his men ashore on Long Island and continued to build up the invasion force until it was double the size of the American opposition in that location.

At first, many of the defenders were not unduly worried. The heart of their fortifications was along the crest of a series of hills in Brooklyn, with the East River and Manhattan behind them. The Americans, remembering their valor at Bunker Hill, believed the British again could be lured into marching uphill into a withering hail of fire.

But General Howe was well aware of Washington's plans, and was not going to allow his men to make the same mistake twice. Rather than trying to storm the main American force, the British cautiously began probing the sides of the defending lines and discovered that some of the flanks were weak. Rushing those points, the British so overwhelmed small clusters of defenders that many surrendered on the spot.

In the forests in front of the heights, American riflemen had been posted to deal with the expected frontal assault. But the enemy approached from the sides, and the riflemen, believing at first that the approaching soldiers were Americans, failed to fire until it was

The Army Is Saved

too late. The advance American positions quickly fell, and the British were upon the main defenses before Washington realized it.

To the commander-in-chief, who arrived on Long Island late in the battle when he finally realized that this was the main British thrust, the situation looked perilous. His soldiers had their backs to the East River, where the British fleet stood ready to cut them off from Manhattan. The British controlled the ground on the other sides, so an overland retreat was impossible. This was the heart of the American army, and its surrender would have meant at least a serious weakening of the revolution, if not the end.

A dirty, tired, dispirited band of 9,500 Americans withdrew to their last remaining position on the heights on August 27, where they awaited the final British attack.[22] The redcoats remained just outside the camp, believing the Americans eventually could be taken without an all-out assault. To add to the Americans' grief, a rainstorm drenched the huddled troops, many of whom were without shelter. All they had for food were biscuits and pickled pork, which had to be eaten raw.

But Washington was not finished. He decided to try to evacuate his force during the night, provided the British fleet did not intervene. He was counting on continuing bad weather to cloak his movements. The man he chose to organize the hazardous operation was the old sea dog, Alexander McDougall, who knew the harbor and its sailors as well or better than anybody else.[23] Having had to sit out most of the action on Long Island while his brigade was held in reserve, he welcomed the chance to be useful. On August 9, he had been promoted to brigadier general by the Continental Congress in recognition of his political contributions, a common occurrence at that time. He set about his task with vigor, even though he at first had counseled in favor of waiting another day or so until the weather cleared. But Washington was anxious to move, so McDougall sent his men, who included many former seamen, back to Manhattan where they galloped on horseback through the city, mustering all the sailors they could find. By nightfall, a large, motley "fleet"—from rowboats to sailing ships—was assembled on the Manhattan side of the East River. As quietly as possible, they pushed off for the opposite shore where the American army was waiting.

That evening, August 29, the Continentals began to break up camp, although they left their fires burning to fool the British. At a ferry boat landing, with General McDougall supervising, ex-fishermen in Glover's and Hutchinson's Regiments from Salem, Massachusetts, helped the soldiers board. Then they rowed silently to Manhattan, where the men were disembarked. Time after time, the crossings were repeated as the night wore on. Only for a short while, when strong winds made the passage too perilous, were the operations suspended. During those tense moments, McDougall sent an officer to inform Washington of the setback. The commander, however, could not be located, and McDougall was left to his own devices. Fortunately, the winds decreased before midnight, and the evacuation resumed.

In the early morning hours, a potentially disastrous situation developed as the result of an inexplicable blunder by an aide to Washington.[24] The officer approached General Thomas Mifflin, whose soldiers were acting as rear guards, and told him his force should proceed immediately to the dock. Mifflin protested, but the aide insisted, so the troops departed, leaving the rear undefended.

En route to the landing, they met Washington, who was shocked by what appeared to be the desertion of some of his best soldiers. "Good God!" Washington exclaimed. "General Mifflin, I am afraid you have ruined us by unseasonably withdrawing the troops from the lines." Mifflin in exasperation explained what had happened, and then returned with his men to their posts. Eventually, they, too, were able to make their escape.

At dawn, the British sent out scouting parties to find out why the American lines were so quiet. They discovered that the whole Army, including men, horses, cannon and biscuits, was gone. They might still have picked up the last soldiers waiting at the dock, but, providentially, a fog settled in and cloaked the remaining boats as they departed. It was, all in all, an amazing performance, and nothing like it would occur until, ironically, the British managed a similar miracle at Dunkerque in 1940.

General Washington had been one of the last to leave Long Island. Gloomy and distraught by the defeat, he took little comfort from the achievement of the night—even though it is now considered one of the most remarkable feats of military history. The historian, Alexander Botta, said no military operation "was ever conducted by a great captain with more ability and prudence." One of England's leading scholars, George Macaulay Trevelyan, called the evacuation "a master stroke of energy, dexterity and caution, by which Washington saved his army and his country."

Although McDougall over the decades has received little public credit for his part, it was undoubtedly one of his greatest contributions to the revolution. At the very least, his expert handling of one of the most difficult logistical operations of the war secured forever the trust and admiration of George Washington.

Against the Odds, 8
They Survived

New York looked like a dying city in the first two weeks of September 1776. The redcoats peered down on Manhattan from the captured heights of Brooklyn, and the British fleet maneuvered incessantly in the harbor. It was only a matter of time, the Americans knew, before the enemy would attack, and there seemed little chance that the discouraged army of Washington would be able to prevent the capture or destruction of the port. Many houses were shut, their inhabitants in the countryside or en route to England, as their sentiments dictated. With commerce at a standstill, most activity was confined to the troops.

Worried and uncertain about the future, McDougall sat down to write his last will and testament.[1] To "my beloved wife, Hannah McDougall," he designated all his household furniture "and a Negro wench called Bett." He divided the remainder of his goods among his wife, son, and daughter.

For the harassed General Washington, it also was a time for agonizing decisions. Although Congress wanted New York defended, many American officers in the city were convinced the situation was hopeless. After several days of hesitation, Washington called a conference of his top commanders at McDougall's home. There the issue was hotly debated—with Washington and General Greene, among others, arguing for evacuation of the city. McDougall evidently agreed, because he later ridiculed General William Heath's arguments in favor of remaining.[2] McDougall snapped that if Heath's advice had been accepted, "his arm would have been white on a gibbet [gallows] before this, and the commander-in-chief and other generals must have shared the same fate." General Thomas Mifflin, McDougall later recalled, "got up and addressed General Heath with much asperity."

Most of the American forces had been moved north of the city proper when the British struck on September 16. The fleet moved swiftly up the East River to Kip's Bay, and bombarded the thin contingent of Americans there. When the redcoats came storming ashore in flat-bottomed landing boats, the defenders, many of whom had seen little or no combat, fled in panic. It was Washington himself who finally halted the flight, using his cane on the hapless deserters. Shouting that he would ram his sword through any man he caught away from his post, he rallied the shaky soldiers only yards from the advancing British. It was long enough to regain order, and the Americans then retreated to safer positions.

The British marched south to the tip of Manhattan, capturing New York City with scarcely a casualty. While the redcoats were celebrating, fires (probably set by remaining patriots) broke out and consumed hundreds of buildings before they were stopped. The port was still a valuable prize, but the blaze made the occupation more crowded and less comfortable than it might have been otherwise.

Washington, who wanted to avoid another full-scale battle, retreated steadily northward over a period of several weeks, arriving at White Plains in late October. The British were not far behind, and it soon became clear that another major confrontation was in the making.

Directly in front of the village of White Plains on October 28, the Americans made their initial stand. They held off repeated attacks by the British and Hessians, but eventually were forced back by the enemy veterans to a defensive position on hills overlooking the town.

A half mile from the righthand side of the main American forces, just across the Bronx River, Washington placed McDougall in command of a 1,600-man group on Chatterton's Hill. The units included McDougall's own First New York Regiment and contingents from Connecticut, Maryland, Delaware, and Massachusetts, many of them unseasoned militiamen. One of the officers under McDougall's command was his young friend, Alexander Hamilton.

The enemy already was bombarding the hill when McDougall arrived. A whole regiment had started to run when one of the men was wounded, and they were restrained only with great difficulty. On the field on the opposite side of the river, the British army was drawing up, in preparation to attack.

"Its appearance was truly magnificent," an American officer related. "A bright autumnal sun shed its luster on the polished arms; and the rich array of dress and military equipage gave an imposing grandeur to the scene as they advanced in all the pomp and circumstance of war."[3]

While some 10,000 British troops stood by, about 4,000 men, backed by a dozen cannon, maneuvered toward the river bank. The guns fired so often that it sounded like a continuous peal of thunder to the beleaguered Americans. The river was high because of storms, and a unit of Hessians refused to cross. An officer ordered the construction of a makeshift bridge, to be made of trees felled on the spot. While the work was going on, a group of Marylanders and New Yorkers descended part way down the hill and fired at the Germans, who were momentarily stunned.

A group of British soldiers, meanwhile, had discovered a ford not far away, and began to cross there. They advanced a short way up the hill, but encountered such heavy fire that they fell back until Hessian reinforcements arrived. The whole attacking force by this time had crossed the stream and were struggling up the steep slope. A unit of Hessians rounded the side of the American lines at about the same time that the light dragoons on horseback appeared in front. Their presence was awesomely announced by kettledrums and trumpets carried by some of the soldiers. It was enough to frighten even a veteran, and some of the inexperienced militiamen, who until then had fought bravely, broke and ran. Many were killed or wounded by the swords of the mounted cavalrymen, and others surrendered.

The remaining Americans, greatly outnumbered, fought on until

McDougall decided it was no use. Colonel John Haslet's Delaware Regiment, the last to leave the hill, effectively held off the British until the other men had retreated. Then they left to join the main American Army a short march away. Between 100 and 300 Americans were killed or wounded. British and Hessian casualties totaled about 200—enough to make them abandon plans to attack Washington's main force.

Many Americans were downhearted at the defeat, but General Lee had another view.[4] "McDougall in the last affair," he declared, "was obliged to retreat by the superiority of their artillery, but he lost no credit—the loss on their side was considerable."

From the British point of view, the spirited resistance of the Americans gave them pause—so much pause, in fact, that a Parliamentary committee was appointed to find out why General Howe had failed to pursue and capture Washington and his army.

The strategy on both sides was becoming clear. Howe wanted to engage in a classic, all-out battle, European-style, in which he believed he had vast superiority over the Americans. Washington understood that he and his underequipped and untrained troops were no match for the British on such grounds. The Virginian preferred to retreat when necessary, fighting only when conditions and terrain were favorable. In that kind of war, the American wilderness was on Washington's side, and he could have dodged and feinted indefinitely in the steep hills of upstate New York.

Howe chose to remain as close as possible to the sea lanes. He partly made up for his lack of success at White Plains by attacking and capturing two American redoubts guarding the Hudson—Fort Washington on Manhattan Island and Fort Lee opposite on the New Jersey side. More than 2,000 Americans surrendered when Fort Washington fell. The loss, which also included some of the Continentals' best cannon and personal weapons, was a serious blow.

In an unsuccessful attempt to trap Washington, Howe pushed into New Jersey, wide open as the result of the capture of Fort Lee, while General Guy Carleton moved south out of Canada. On Lake Champlain, Carleton defeated an improvised American "fleet" of log rafts, built under the direction of General Benedict Arnold, but the battle delayed the British just enough to make them reconsider pushing on through the wilderness with winter approaching.

Against the Odds, They Survived

Washington, meanwhile, shifted his army into northern New Jersey, sometimes only a few steps ahead of the redcoats. By December it was clear that the Americans would not be able to hold much of the province, and might also lose Philadelphia, where Congress was meeting. To many, the British seemed invincible, and spirits sank even lower when Newport, Rhode Island, was captured without a fight.

Washington managed at last to stall the redcoats on the banks of the Delaware River. Because it was late in the season, General Howe retired to the comforts of New York for the winter, leaving small detachments at various strongholds across New Jersey. Washington, fearful of an offensive up the Hudson which would cut his army in half, left behind a force at Morristown, New Jersey, to protect the rear.

Morale sank to a low point among the Americans. Many of Washington's men, who had enlisted for a limited period, wanted to go home, believing that all was lost. McDougall, who because of ill health had remained with the supporting forces at Morristown, was so despondent that he considered resigning his commission.[5] Washington replied to McDougall's suggestion with this note: "I think with you that though your state of health may require a resignation that this is not a proper time to make it. Our enemies would probably attribute it to the late unfavorable aspect of our affairs, and therefore I would advise you to try whether a little rest might not contribute to the cure of a disorder which is generally brought on by colds and fatigue."

It was evident to Washington that something must be done quickly to raise his countrymen's spirits, and he proceeded with uncharacteristic boldness on Christmas Day. Crossing the ice-laden Delaware in small boats, he and his men pounced on a drunken force of Hessians who had overcelebrated the holiday in Trenton. Washington himself described this famous scene in a letter to McDougall:

> I crossed over to Jersey the evening of the 25th about 9 miles above Trenton with upwards of 2,000 men and attacked three regiments of Hessians consisting of fifteen hundred men, about 8 o'clock next morning. Our men pushed on with such rapidity that they soon carried four pieces of cannon out of six, sur-

rounded the enemy and obliged 30 officers and 886 privates to lay down their arms without firing a shot. Our loss was only two officers and two or three privates wounded."[6]

The countersign picked for the battle by Washington was "victory or death," the motto of the McDougall clan.

Washington said that he hoped that the success of the venture "and the consequences of it will change the face of matters not only there [at McDougall's quarters] but everywhere else." The commander-in-chief urged McDougall "to collect a body of men to be ready to join me, or act otherwise as occasion may be."

Washington also noted that he had sought the exchange of McDougall's son, Ranald Stephen, and certain other prisoners for British captives, but that General Howe had turned over an entirely different group.

"I have remonstrated to him upon this head," the Virginian said, "and have assured him that I will send in no more prisoners till he sends out the paroles of the officers taken in Canada."

Washington's personal concern for the captured young officer continued after his release a few weeks later. Young McDougall, temporarily a civilian, remained with his father until a commission could be secured for him. General McDougall observed that he did not want his son to become "a useless pensioner," and informed Washington that he was keeping his son "attentive to brigade duty and reading." The commander-in-chief thereupon placed the young man in command of a company, commenting: "The part he early took in the contest and his sufferings for it would not be rewarded was he to be neglected."[7]

The youth served for much of the remainder of the war as an aide to his father. The general also had the company of his wife, Hannah, during much of the revolution, although she occasionally lived elsewhere in rented houses when he was traveling.

McDougall's main assignment throughout the war was defending the wild shores of the Hudson against British attacks—some real, some threatened. A never-ending source of worry to Washington was that the redcoats would succeed in cutting the country in half by taking the river with forces from Canada and New York. With

Against the Odds, They Survived

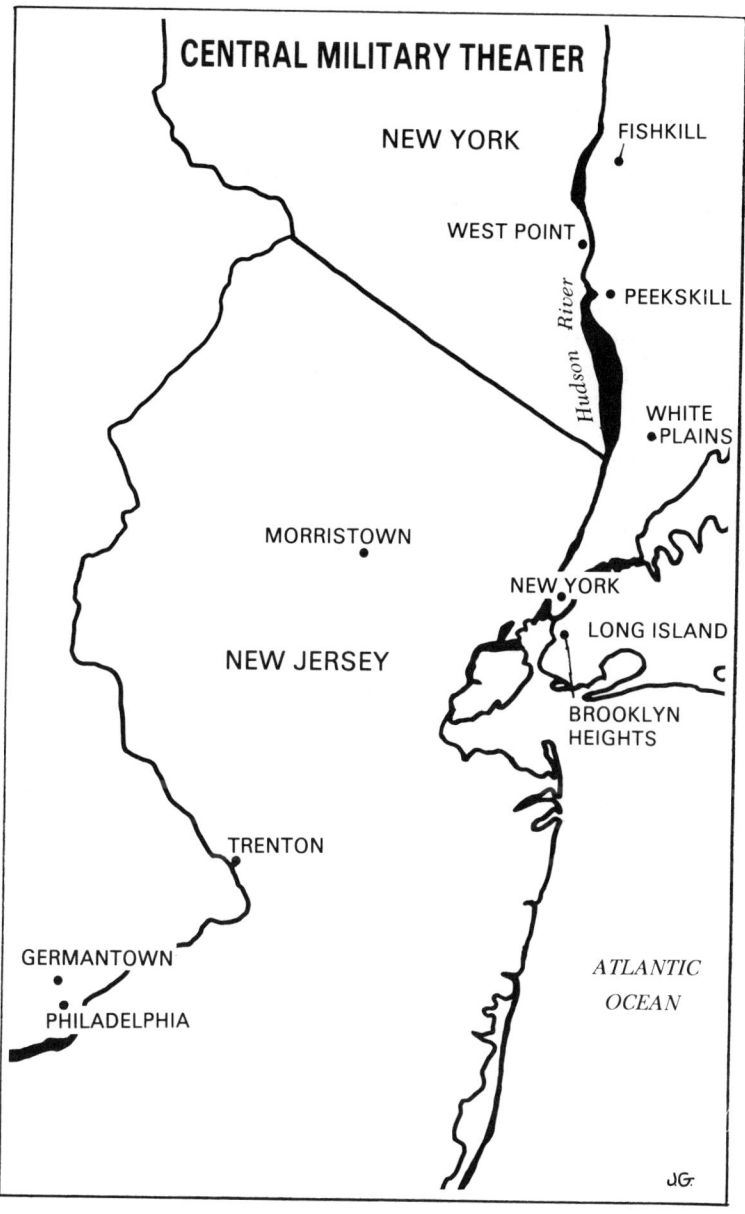

the Royal Navy in command of the sea, communications between New England and the rest of the colonies would be virtually ended and the cause probably lost.

McDougall's orders from the commander-in-chief were to strengthen the fortifications all along the river as best he could. Materials were scarce, and the remnants of army units he had inherited were ragged, hungry and few in number, hardly up to the task of preventing an invasion. The officer complained that he had fewer than 600 men to garrison three forts, secure the overland passes in the region, defend the town of Peekskill where large quantities of supplies were located, and protect the inhabitants of the area.[8]

McDougall informed Washington that "we have not five days provisions of meat at this post [Peekskill]" and the troops from Massachusetts "are almost naked and will soon become sickly for want of shirts."[9] He declared that "the health of the troops as well as the reputation of the Continent require their having speedy relief."

The countryside around him was seething with civil disorder.[10] Pro-British settlers were feeding the British with both information and provisions while Americans often went hungry. McDougall noted that the residents of western Westchester County were "so disaffected that no aid can be expected from them."

Typical, he said, was the case of a group of Tories in the nearby mountains whose houses "serve as rendezvous and hiding places for the recruits of the enemy. The safety of the community, in my opinion, requires the families to be removed and the houses to be destroyed. The barn of the chairman of the [pro-revolutionary] subcommittee for this quarter was set on fire at night three days ago. From the time and circumstances of it, I am persuaded it was done by some enemy to the country."

In dealing with both civil and military matters, McDougall was a harsh disciplinarian. He had, for example, a hand in the court martial of Simon Mabee, who was accused of spying for the British.

"When he was brought before me," McDougall noted, "he had great appearance of guilt, which is a faithful index to the heart."[11]

Mabee was sentenced "to be hanged by the neck until dead."

In a similar fashion, McDougall approved of the death sentence for four soldiers who had been convicted of desertion. The officer explained: "There have been so many instances of that kind in this department, exemplary and the severest punishment are become necessary."[12] The general added that the sentence was to be carried out "with the utmost tenderness to the unhappy prisoners."

At a time when many families were separated because of the British occupation, he was often asked by fathers or sons for permission to cross enemy lines to visit their loved ones. If a citizen could show good reason, he usually was given a "flag of truce," and it was ordinarily honored by the other side for temporary passage.

McDougall was therefore miffed when the British detained Cornelius Bogert, whom the officer had allowed to return to his family's farm in Harlem to locate some financial vouchers.[13] In a letter to the British commander in New York City, the general heatedly demanded to know why Bogert had been jailed.

"If he has not acted with that formality or delicacy which he ought to have observed," McDougall declared, "it must be owing to his ignorance, for I do not think him hardy enough if it had been proposed to him to act in the character of a spy."

A British officer replied that Bogert "was confined as a suspected person for coming opposite to Harlem and making a signal for a boat by tying a rag to a stick. You must be sensible he came in an improper and uncommon way, and that no regard ought to be paid to such suspicious flags. General Howe has released him some days ago at the request of his friends, and I believe you will not find that he has felt any severity but that of confinement. I wish that friends to [British] government at no time experienced greater hardships, but we have heard of many instances of their being marched in irons through the country by those under your command."[14]

Time consuming as they were, such duties were secondary to McDougall's primary task of safeguarding the Hudson. On Washington's orders, the supply base at Peekskill was expanded with a variety of materials intended as a reserve for the main army. Unfortunately, the location, along the Hudson only about forty miles from British headquarters, proved to be a poor choice. It was an easy journey up river for the Royal Navy, and when General Howe discovered how poorly defended the depot was, he determined to take it. One of his first steps was to try to put McDougall off guard. Within hearing of an American officer taken prisoner at Fort Washington, the British outlined a fictitious plan of attack.[15] Knowing full well the officer would report what he had heard, the British then released the American to his countrymen at Peekskill.

McDougall, after hearing the report, said he doubted its authenticity because the British had spoken of their plan so publicly. The general, nevertheless, did what he could to prepare his 250-man force at the depot, dispersing supplies including rum, sugar, molasses, and candles, as fast as possible to other locations. But before he finished, ten British ships sailed up the Hudson and anchored off Peekskill. On a fine March afternoon, 800 redcoats landed at a cove a mile and a half from the depot, bringing with them four pieces of artillery.

"From the numbers of boats which were filled with men, the force of the enemy was unquestionably far superior to ours," McDougall explained to Washington. The New Yorker waited for the enemy on a hill behind the town. The British advanced to an opposite hill and formed for an attack. "There I was fully satisfied of their great superiority," McDougall reported, "and whenever the heavy artillery had got some distance in my rear, I ordered the troops to retire in good order to the passes in the highlands, which they obeyed. The enemy cannonaded us, but we suffered only the loss of one man mortally wounded."

On the following day, American reinforcements arrived from Fort Constitution, led by Lieutenant Colonel Marinus Willett, a cabinet maker who had been active in the Sons of Liberty. While one detachment attempted to divert the British, Willett's group quietly approached the enemy's flank, hoping to surprise them. Part of Willett's group, however, fired too soon, spoiling the surprise.

Willett, according to McDougall, "pressed on, fired smartly on them, ordered his men to fix bayonets, on hearing which the enemy fled with great precipitation to the main body. They were panic struck, asserted the woods were full of rebel soldiers, ascribed our attack to reinforcement, formed on the hill above the town, and lay on their arms till the moon rose, and embarked, leaving a great part of their plunder and the most of our stores undestroyed behind. The enemy had nine killed and wounded, as the townsmen inform us in this skirmish. We also killed four of them whose graves we found near the creek in attempting to burn all our boats. Thus we got rid of these disturbers of our peace."

McDougall confessed to Washington that he found the whole affair "mortifying"—even though the Americans, considering their disadvantages, had performed reasonably well.

Washington replied from Morristown that he regretted the incident, but added that he had "feared that it would be the case, and that their retreat would be effected before a sufficient force could be assembled to cut them off, or to give 'em any great annoyance."[16] The commander-in-chief concluded that "your conduct in marching with the troops from Peekskill under the circumstances you mention was perfectly right and what I wished, and your return, after you found you could not come up with the enemy, was equally judicious, in my opinion."

Some of McDougall's subordinates did not regard the incident with such equanimity. There was considerable grumbling that the affair had been handled badly, and one officer, Colonel Henry B. Livingston, allegedly called the retreat a "scandal." The officer was the politically powerful second son of a prominent judge, Robert R. Livingston, with whose family McDougall had sided early in the revolutionary struggle.

McDougall was disturbed about reports that Colonel Livingston was maligning him to other officers. At length, Livingston was arrested and ordered to a court martial on charges which included slandering his superior. At his trial, he presented an eloquent defense.

"I now address myself to you," Livingston declared, "as the awful tribunal whose judgment will determine not only my cause but the fate of all men of honor in like circumstances—consequently feel a dread upon my spirits when I consider the importance of the subject, the power of my accuser, the many disadvantages this kind of trial naturally subjects me to, and my want of abilities to state in its true light the unbounded malice and insufferable arrogance of my disingenuous accuser."[17]

The officer noted that he had been charged with "traducing the conduct of Brigadier General McDougall in ordering the retreat of the Continental troops" in the Peekskill skirmish. The only evidence, he said, was offered by McDougall's aide, Major Platt, who had heard a secondhand version of a purported conversation in which Livingston had denounced the retreat. The colonel continued: "I might possibly have said it was scandalous to retreat, having never had occasion to retreat before, but that I ever attempted to infer that General McDougall was inferior to other generals or that he had not been vigilant and careful in doing his duty or that he was wanting in abilities, I do utterly deny."

Livingston also was charged with having failed to march his regiment, which he said had no ammunition, to Peekskill at the proper time. The colonel observed that two months had passed since the raid, and he had not been previously punished or reprimanded in any way—as might have been expected if the warrant carried any weight.

McDougall, the colonel asserted, "will cover his malice with a show of humanity and tenderness. Probably he will tell you that regard for my family and numerous connections had induced him to overlook many of my faults, but that I grew so insolent upon indulgence that at length, much against his inclinations, he has been under the disagreeable necessity of arresting me—that he's extremely sorry to treat any gentleman with so much severity; it's the first time, and he hopes it will be the last."

Livingston said he had been treated disrespectfully so many times that he was at last driven to write a letter of protest to General Washington. On one occasion, he recalled, he had delivered a report on the status of his regiment which McDougall considered improperly completed. He quoted the general as remarking: "Do you dare look me in the face and say you had my leave to make out these returns so?"

Livingston replied that he had, with the general's permission. According to Livingston, McDougall answered: "'You tell an abominable lie,' followed me out on his piazza, clenched his fist and placed it for some time in a threatening posture within half an inch of my nose, asserted I was a pest to this army, that I had been more trouble to him than all the army put together, that I had done more hurt in ten days than I should be able to do good in my whole life.

"Although I had armed myself with patience, I could contain myself no longer. I told him his assertions were false, on which I was ordered under arrest."

Livingston concluded his defense with an oration comparing McDougall's actions with "the despotism we have been struggling to oppose." Some of the court, he observed, may have considered the colonel's assertions too bold against a superior officer. But respect dies, Livingston said, when "a man gives way to ungovernable passion and descends from the dignity of his station to such language and actions as are only in use among the lowest of mankind."

The court was impressed by his arguments, although not totally convinced, and Livingston was let off with a reprimand.[18] The finding concluded "that though the colonel appears to this court to be guilty of great imprudence and indiscretion in some parts of his language and conduct towards the general, yet his conduct was not such as will warrant the appellation of being unbecoming a gentleman and an officer."

Livingston's measured restraint did not last long. Shortly after the trial, he sent a note to McDougall challenging him to a duel.[19] The message concluded: "The colonel will be at his quarters tomorrow evening when, if General McDougall will do him the honor to ride with him, he will endeavor to settle a point the court martial have left undetermined."

At about the same time, Livingston circulated copies of an "anonymous" tract, which contained a furious attack on the general's background. It stated:

> I have known a poor, contemptible, mean, half-starved Scotchman when working by daily labor for his daily support in the capacity of a sailor to have so sensible an impression of the lowliness of his station that when passing a person who appeared to be above him in circumstances, was glad to lift his hat as a mark of obeisance while his other hand was employed in preventing the companions of his morning, evening and noontide hours from disturbing his noxious parts of his filthy and infected person.

> I have paused awhile on his condition, viewed him as a man, felt for him as a suffering creature and have been anxiously studious to relieve him from his unhappy situation.[20]

The author observed that he had followed McDougall's way through life from sailor to captain of a privateer, but that the officer remained "rough as his profession" and "mean as the meanest" of the Scots.

Livingston criticized McDougall for having spent his money freely in a vain attempt to become a gentleman. The end result was described as only "some foolish foppery of dress." The general also was cited for trying to "guide the helm of state, and puffed up with pride and persuaded by his partners, the banditti of the town, he takes up the pen and commences one of the scribblers of the age."

The note, raging to the point of hysteria, concluded:

> May we not with propriety think he would stoop to any office, do as his ancestors have done before him, sell milk by the quart, betray and dispose of his Maker like another Jew, ask to make a penny and seek the salvation with this only hope—that a want of soul may prevent the damnation of his body.[21]

McDougall coolly replied that "had the colonel behaved becoming his character while under arrest, the General would have gratified this desire to ride with him this or any other evening. But it would be no honor to the colonel to ride with one 'meaner than the meanest of the race' nor safe for him to be in the evening with one [who would] betray or dispose of his Maker like another Indian."[22]

A copy of the note was sent to General George Clinton with the observation from McDougall that it was almost unimaginable coming from a man with Livingston's "pretended delicacy of manners."[23]

"Poor boy," McDougall noted. "If he knew how little pain his scribbling gave me, he would have saved himself the trouble of composing it."

Soon afterward, Livingston's regiment was detached from McDougall's command and marched northward to join General Schuyler. For distinguished services in the southern campaign later in the war, the irascible colonel was awarded a sword by an Act of Congress.

As the summer drew to a close, the main scene of battle was shifting to New Jersey and Pennsylvania. McDougall was ordered to move to the northern New Jersey hills, where he would be more readily available if the British advanced farther toward Philadelphia.

On September 19, 1777, McDougall received these instructions from a very worried General Washington.[24] "The exigencies of our affairs," the commander-in-chief said, "makes it necessary you should use all the diligence and dispatch in your power to join the Army with the troops under your command. The enemy are making the most vigorous efforts to proceed in their attempt upon Philadelphia, and it will require our utmost exertions to disappoint them. We shall this day cross the Schuykill at Parkers Ford about thirty miles from Philadelphia. The most convenient place for you to cross the Delaware in the present situation of things is Coryels Ferry, but you will govern yourself in this according to circumstances."

Weeks before, McDougall had arrived in the Jersey stronghold with a 900-man brigade as ordered by Washington. The Virginian, as early as May, had begun to fear a two-pronged attack on his scattered forces by General Guy Carleton out of Canada and General Howe operating from New York City. Washington had asked McDougall to tap his intelligence sources on Manhattan, including American sympathizers there, for information.[25]

"I beg you," Washington wrote, "to take every possible means in your power to find out the designs of the enemy and what their plan of operation is. Do not hesitate at expense. I know your own pains will not be wanting. There is a report that General Carleton is on the lakes or pressing down. Whether it is authentic, I cannot say. But if he means an attack on Ticonderoga, I am persuaded General Howe will not go to Philadelphia, but will endeavor to cooperate with him. . . ."

The information was incorrect. General Carleton, who had lost favor in London, was being replaced by General "Gentleman Johnny" Burgoyne, a daring soldier who was a favorite both with his troops and the ladies. Washington was, however, right in one respect—the British were planning another attack on the province of New York, and Burgoyne's first objective was Ticonderoga. It should have been a formidable obstacle.[26] There were 5,000 American soldiers there. But they had failed to secure a hill overlooking the fort, and the British managed to drag two cannon to the top. Faced with the threat of heavy bombardment, the rebels fled—many all the way to their homes in New England.

Burgoyne then began a long march through the forested hills toward Albany. Somewhere in that vicinity, he believed, he would join forces with Howe pushing up from the south, thereby cutting the colonies in half.

But the British commander in New York City had ideas of his own, and the capture of the American capital, Philadelphia, was high on his list of priorities. He and his army sailed out of New York in July, and by the most circuitous of routes, landed in late August at Head of Elk at the northern tip of Chesapeake Bay. Many of Howe's soldiers were fatigued and made ill by the long voyage through wilting summer heat.

News of a preliminary sharp clash between Howe and Washington reached McDougall by way of General Israel Putnam at Peekskill, who had been informed by the commander-in-chief that "our loss has been inconsiderable. It appears the enemy suffered much. They were routed in the forenoon. But by a forced march afterwards, they crossed the Brandywine six miles on his Excellency's [Washington's] right, and moving in great force against part of our Army, caused a retreat." Putnam reported that "our troops were in high spirits after the business was over" and noted that Washington "hopes to give a better account in the next action."[27]

Washington realized that a full-scale battle with Howe was inevitable, and he called in all the reinforcements he could get. McDougall was to bring all he could spare, and more than 2,000 others were summoned from other sectors.

The British also were on the move, and the American command was anxious about their intentions. On September 22, Washington dispatched a rider to McDougall, who was proceeding across New Jersey, to warn him that the redcoats might try to cut him off.

"From the present complexion of affairs," Washington advised, "you should proceed on the most direct route to Pots Grove, nine miles above this place." The Virginian concluded that "I shall not add more than to urge your unremitted diligence to join me as early as possible, assuring you that your aid is extremely wanted and cannot arrive too soon."[28]

Two days later, however, Washington sent another dispatch, warning that he was worried that the enemy might be in a position "to interrupt your march which I think they can and surely will do if they have any good advice of your approach—and of this I have no doubt, as we are in a most disaffected country."[29]

Washington advised McDougall to change his route, and the New Yorker complied, arriving at the main camp without serious incident. The American forces totaling about 11,000 drew up sixteen miles north of Germantown, a pleasant village just northwest of Philadelphia.[30] The hamlet consisted mainly of two rows of houses facing each other along a hilly, wooded road leading from Philadelphia to Reading. About the only building of any consequence was the two-and-a-half story graystone Georgian mansion built as a summer retreat for Benjamin Chew, the chief justice of Pennsylvania. At the time of the battle, Chew, accused of loyalty to the King, was under arrest in New Jersey.

In and around the village were General Howe and his army of about 9,000, much smaller than normal. Hundreds of other redcoats had been dispatched to help clear a safe passage for British ships up the Delaware River. The effort was considered necessary to keep the Philadelphia area well supplied, since overland routes were controlled for the most part by the Americans.

For once, the numerically superior continentals agreed, the time was ripe for attack. Washington's plan was to divide his forces into four main columns, two of which would attack the center of the British line while the other two groups would flank the redcoats and attack them from the rear. It was a brilliant plan, classic in its approach to battle, but complicated by distance and the lack of communication among the American forces.

McDougall was assigned to flank the strongest contingent, commanded by General Greene. This group, comprising more than half the army, was supposed to attack the principal British forces near Howe's headquarters. McDougall's orders, dated October 3, contained these notes: "The troops to be ready at 6 o'clock this evening . . . General McDougall to march in front of the troops that compose the left wing and file off to attack the enemy's right flank."[31]

The center columns, which had started their exhausting march at dusk the night before, were the first to meet the outlying British positions at dawn, and the redcoats stubbornly resisted before superior numbers forced them back toward their main camp. As often happens in the autumn in that area, there was a heavy mist hanging low over the roads and fields, and visibility decreased even more when the gunfire began.

Under fog cover, a number of redcoats assembled in the sturdy Chew house, along the road over which the Americans were proceeding. There the British fired from windows at the enemy, most of whom were able to slip by without difficulty.

When a reserve force in which Washington was marching approached the embattled house, the chief of artillery, Brigadier General Henry Knox, advised against permitting even this small pocket of resistance to remain, thus endangering the American rear. It now seems clear the house was little more than an annoyance, but a substantial number of soldiers who should have been proceeding toward the main British line were detoured to attack the mansion. Attempts to destroy it with cannonading and burning failed, and the redcoats were able to hold the house despite overwhelming odds. The mansion stands intact today, bearing only a few relatively minor scars to remind visitors of the violence that engulfed it two centuries ago.

As General Greene's powerful force approached the British center on another road, the noise of the Chew house battle reached General Adam Stephen. Without orders to do so, Stephen pulled his men out of Greene's column and began bombarding the house with heavy guns. The sudden increase in noise alarmed General Anthony Wayne, who mistakenly thought the British were reinforcing their men at Chew house. In a ghastly tragedy of errors, Wayne's men were taken by Stephen's forces to be enemies, and the fog-shrouded American contingents began battling each other. In the confusion, both groups panicked and started to run from each other.

Greene, meanwhile, pressed on with McDougall's brigade and those of the fighting Lutheran minister, General Peter Muhlenberg, and General Charles Scott.[32] Despite stiff resistance, the column forged ahead and broke through the British center at the market house. Muhlenberg's men fixed bayonets and advanced as far as the main British encampment, where many redcoats were taken prisoner amid their tents. Officers on both sides thought at that moment the Americans had won. The British lines were in such confusion that some officers talked about retreating to reform again at Chester, fifteen miles to the rear.

At about that time, however, General John Sullivan's division which was the remaining part of the American center was forcefully attacked by a British brigade and thrown off balance. Hearing the fearful sound of bombardment at Chew house behind them, they became convinced they were surrounded. Suddenly, the men broke and ran, leaving Greene without allies on his right or left. The redcoats were reinforced by the men who had been engaging Sullivan; and Greene, Scott, and McDougall found themselves on the defensive. Muhlenberg's men, behind the enemy lines, whirled about and fought their way back to their own lines.

Exhausted by the long march and ferocious fighting, Greene's column began to pull back, delaying the enemy by darting in and out of protective fence lines and hedgerows. Theirs was mainly an orderly retreat, although some were running at full speed. Washington himself tried to hold the army in check, but the men would have none of it. Some of the men were out of ammunition, and others too tired to care. Several officers were discovered asleep, and another—Stephen—was found drunk beside a fence. McDougall, at one point, stumbled across a group of Maryland militiamen dozing at the side of the road. Get up, he shouted, or he would fire at them.[33]

A journal among McDougall's papers, which he himself may have written, described the heartbreak felt by the Americans who had believed for a moment they had "obtained a glorious and complete victory. Unfortunately, the morning of the attack, there was a very thick fog. That and the smoke, owing to the constant and live fire kept up by our troops and to a strategy of the enemy burning dry buckwheat and the wind being in their favor, made it impossible to see . . . which caused our troops to get into some confusion, and a retreat took place when the enemy recovered."[34]

The journal concluded: "Our men behaved with the greatest spirit and bravery and deserved the victory they were so near of having which would have given General Howe's army a blow as no doubt would have secured peace."

After the battle, the American forces headed wearily northwest and made camp near what is today the community of Ambler, about eight miles from Germantown.

Washington had information that the British were sending a convoy of supplies to their troops from Chester, and he sent McDougall out with a "flying column"—a small, mobile force of men—to see if they could intercept and capture the material.[35] On a bitterly cold and wet night, they prowled the countryside in a vain search for the enemy. Finally, chilled to the bone, they returned to camp at Barren Hill. During the march, the squad was forced to wade a stream, and, soaked to the waists, the men were chilled even further as their clothes froze in the biting wind. They set out again the next night, but discovered that the redcoats had left the area, and the search was abandoned.

McDougall then accompanied Greene to New Jersey to harass Lord Cornwallis whose army was rounding up cattle and supplies for the winter. The British general, however, retired to Philadelphia for the season. The Americans promptly returned to their main camp at Whitemarsh, north of Philadelphia.

Night after night, the Americans sat in their frigid tents discussing the battle, and how it almost had turned the tide. Whether or not, as some of them thought, Germantown could have ended the war is open to question, but the battle did have long-term consequences. The Americans realized that, despite their best efforts, they were not yet a match in classical warfare for the disciplined British army. At the same time, General Howe, shaken by his narrow escape, would never again take the rebel forces lightly. It was thus ordained that the war would go on inconclusively for several more seasons.

Arguments continued to flare over the conduct of various individuals in the battle. General Greene, among others, was severely criticized, and he called on McDougall for support. "You will oblige me very much with your opinion (with the candor of a friend) respecting my conduct that day," the officer wrote. "I wish to know whether I showed a want of activity in carrying the troops on to action, or want of judgment in the disposition, or want of spirit in the action or retreat."[36]

McDougall, who had returned to Morristown, replied that he "did not see the least indication of your want of activity or spirit in carrying on the troops that day, but the contrary. Those of your and General Stephen's divisions marched so brisk or ran to the charge that they were some minutes out of sight of my brigade, although we formed and marched immediately behind your division when its rear passed the corner of the fence where the new disposition was made. And as to the retreat, your endeavors were not wanting to bring off the troops in order, but could not effect it as the panic had seized them, and your conduct was far from showing any sign of fear."[37]

As to his part in the battle, McDougall was credited for having conducted his men gallantly, making up amply for any ill feeling that might have remained after the Peekskill affair. Washington recommended to Congress that the New Yorker be promoted to major general, the highest rank under commander-in-chief, and a station shared by only a relatively few Continental soldiers.

"From his abilities, military knowledge, and approved bravery," Washington stated, "he has every claim to promotion. If I mistake not, he was passed over in the last appointments of major generals, and younger officers preferred before him; but his disinterested attachment to the service prevented him acting in the manner that is customary in like circumstances."[38]

His promotion, quickly approved by Congress, was dated October 20, 1777. There was also good news from the northern fighting front: "Gentleman Johnny" Burgoyne had surrendered at Saratoga, New York, worn down as the result of incessant attacks by the rebels as the redcoats marched through the forests. It was the first major victory of the war for the Americans, and a welcome antidote for the disappointment at Germantown.

The Cabal   9

A lonely young naval officer, John McDougall, sought a friendly word of encouragement from his Uncle Alexander during the bleak winter of early 1778. From his warship at Charleston, South Carolina, the youth lamented:

> I have wrote so many letters to my relatives since the *Randolph* first arrived in this port (which is now almost a twelve month ago) without receiving a single line in return or so much as the satisfaction of knowing whether either of them ever reached their hands that I despair of ever having that pleasure. . . [it] makes me feel myself alone in the world. My relations are few but very dear to me and to be entirely neglected and unnoted by them gives me so much uneasiness that I cannot help mentioning it.[1]

Lieutenant McDougall boasted of having helped in the capture of enemy shipping which had turned out to be a rich prize. His share amounted to a princely £10,000 which he said was far more than he was accustomed to handling.

"I have, however, disposed of £4,000 of it," he observed, "in the purchase of a good brick house and lot in a very good stand that now rents for £295 a year."

The young man, who had entrusted some of the money to his uncle, asked the general to spend some of the funds on a delicate private matter which both men evidently understood but was not spelled out in the letter.

"I would wish Betsey Hamilton to have as much of it as you think necessary," John said. "Poor girl. I have not heard a breath of her neither since I saw her fifteen months ago."

John also had distressing news of his brother, Alexander.

"I saw a master of a vessel this morning who gave me the following disagreeable account of my brother," he related. "He says he came on board his vessel in Martinique about three weeks ago and asked for a passage which he was made welcome to. After telling him his name, he knew him and recollected to have seen him in New York. Told him he left his brother in Charleston but three weeks before, at which he seemed highly pleased—but was bare of clothes. The man divided with him. Two or three days after that, he had occasion to go ashore in the boat to water—left the coat, pawned the clothes the man had given him for that which I am sorry to say he used to like so well, and went on board another vessel bound to Baltimore. . . ."

Lieutenant McDougall commented that "the Lord knows what will become" of his brother, who "will never be better. I rejoiced when I first heard of him and expected to have had an opportunity of dividing my little all with him." But as the result of what he learned, John said, he wished "never to see him."

The youth continued that "I cannot close this letter without begging your acceptance of the unfeigned acknowledgments of a heart truly grateful for the many obligations I am under to you. Every word I write and every little advantage or happiness I enjoy in life if possible heightens the sense I have of them."

A few days later, the *Randolph*—"well manned, equipped and ready for sea again"—sailed out of Charleston, never to return. It was blown up in battle, and John McDougall, along with many other sailors, was killed. It was still another personal loss for General McDougall, for whom the war was beginning to seem endless and without much hope of success.

Forced by a "severe nervous fever" to leave the main army and seek medical help, he wrote to Washington from Morristown in

The Cabal

February that his "health is now perfectly restored, but I cannot say the same for my strength. Every experiment I make to ascertain it convinces me of the want of it. I have not yet ventured on horseback. But, notwithstanding, I hope soon to be in a condition for duty. If in the meantime there should be a pressing call for me in the army, I will repair to it whenever your Excellency pleases to signify it."[2]

The call, which would involve McDougall in one of the most heated controversies of the war, was soon to come. It had been an extraordinarily grim winter for most American soldiers. George Washington and his ill-clothed men, huddled among the hills at Valley Forge, were often on the verge of starvation. They were woefully short of tents and blankets, and the death of hundreds of horses made it next to impossible to haul supplies from the modest farms nearby. What made it seem especially scandalous was that life elsewhere in the country, particularly among civilians, carried on much the same as ever. Tables in the homes of thousands of Americans were heaped with steaks, potatoes, and cakes. In occupied Philadelphia, the redcoats were becoming fat. Plays, concerts and parties filled the evenings of many a soldier, often accompanied by some of the city's pretty loyalist ladies. General Howe's reluctance to take to the field during the cold months was ascribed to his fondness for his attentive American mistress.

At the same time, some members of Congress were becoming disturbed by Washington's increasing popularity. While thousands of his countrymen considered the craggy-faced Virginian the symbol of American virtue, others feared he might use his power to seize dictatorial power of the fledgling nation. Benjamin Rush, a Philadelphia doctor who was a member of Congress, was among those who distrusted the commander-in-chief.

Within the army, too, there were a number of high-ranking officers who, for their own reasons, believed Washington should be replaced. This group included General Horatio Gates, the hero of Saratoga, long critical of Washington's military abilities, and Brigadier General Thomas Conway, an Irishman who had served in the French army before joining the American forces. Conway, able and ambitious, was anxious for promotion to major general. The Irishman had criticized Washington for being unable to make up his mind during the Germantown battle, and the Virginian, who had heard of Conway's remarks, was dead set against the promotion.

Conway wrote to Gates suggesting that Gates might be a welcome successor to Washington as head of the army. When a gossipy aide to Gates disclosed the suggestion, Washington's allies were shocked and rallied to his side against the "cabal."

Congress, which had been ousted from Philadelphia by the British, was meeting for the winter in York, Pennsylvania. The majority of members, however, were home for the season, and a relatively few delegates were running the show. It was this group, despite Washington's objections, which approved Conway's promotion. Also approved was the upgrading of the Board of War, an arm of Congress designed to serve as liaison between the lawmakers and the soldiers. The members previously were drawn from Congress, which meant that it actually did very little because each legislator was busy with other affairs.

Under the revised scheme, active military officers were appointed to the board, which, at least theoretically, superseded Washington at the head of the army. The choices of Congress to serve on the board appeared to be a direct slap at Washington. Gates was named president, Conway was selected as inspector general, and General Thomas Mifflin, also considered unfriendly to Washington, was appointed as an adviser.

One of the board's first actions was to draw up plans for another invasion of Canada, a proposal which many other officers regarded as senseless. Gates, however, was convinced it would work, especially if headed by the young Marquis de Lafayette. It was supposed that the dashing Frenchman would be able to address the French Canadians in their own tongue, thereby making them more sympathetic to the American cause. Congress approved the plan before according Washington even the courtesy of commenting on it. By that time, the Virginian was convinced that the "cabal" was real, and that Gates and certain members of Congress were out to get him.

The commander, however, was still warmly supported by the majority of his officers and enlisted men, even in their misery at Valley Forge. One of his greatest admirers was Lafayette, a distinguished nobleman who had rushed to America at the outbreak of war to accept a commission as major general. The Frenchman reluctantly agreed to head the expedition to Canada, but only if he could discard the Congressional choice for second-in-command, Conway, and pick his own deputy. His choice, upon the advice of fellow officers at Valley Forge, was McDougall—a steady, loyal, and mature officer who was acquainted with much of the terrain and a magician in providing logistical support even when supplies were scarce.

Lafayette explained to Congress that he wanted McDougall because of "his rigid and imperturbable virtue." When the legislators balked at his demands, he threatened to return to France with the foreign officers he had recruited—a move that almost certainly would have upset American efforts to persuade France to enter the war.[3] The politicians capitulated.

Lafayette wrote to McDougall: "Congress, desiring an incursion is made into Canada, has appointed me to the command of that body of troops. General Conway and General Kalb were appointed to go with me, but I have expressed my earnest desire of going with you, and Congress has at length granted this point." Lafayette observed that the object of the expedition was to go north on the ice to St. Johns and Montreal and try to win the affections of the Canadian people. "I have not, sir, the pleasure of being long acquainted with you," the Frenchman concluded, "but your reputation in every respect and what I know and I have seen or heard myself from you make me look upon your presence as very necessary."[4]

McDougall was flattered, but told friends he was unconvinced of the wisdom of conducting such a campaign. He explained to Lafayette that "it's out of my power to gratify your wishes. . . . Although my health is restored, such is the state of my strength that I cannot flatter myself my going with you into Canada would advance the service, for strength is necessary in a soldier to endure the fatigue of the excursion mentioned."[5] In the end, the expedition was called off because so many doubts had been raised, and Lafayette had lost what little enthusiasm he had originally had for the mission. Lafayette, who had been consulting with McDougall and others, returned to the main army.

Some have doubted that a "cabal" ever really existed, but Washington's strongest supporters, including McDougall and Greene, were convinced there was. They were incensed by criticism of Washington's leadership in the Battle of Germantown, and particularly resentful of Conway's remarks that the Virginian had been bewildered and unable to make up his mind. Conway, on the other hand, called McDougall "one of the best heads in the Army."

From Valley Forge, Greene—noting that the Army "has been greatly convulsed"—wrote to McDougall about Conway's appointment to major general:

> I think him a very dangerous man in this Army. . . . He has but small talents—great ambition—and without any uncommon spirit of enterprise, naturally of a factious make and of an intriguing temper. It is said (and I don't doubt the truth of it) that he wrote to General Gates that he believed God Almighty favored the American Army or else they must have been destroyed, aided by such an ignorant council that did not fall a sacrifice. Can you believe it?
>
> This gentleman is puffed off to the public as one of the greatest generals of the age. . . . This is done by a certain faction that is said to be forming under the auspices of General Gates and General Mifflin to supplant his Excellency from the command of the Army and get General Gates at the head of it. How success swells the vanity of the human heart. This gentleman is a mere child of fortune.[6]

McDougall replied that he found Conway's promotion "neither just nor politic." He noted that he had served with the Irishman, and "could not observe any extraordinary marks of military genius about him."[7] McDougall was aghast at the thought of having Washington removed from his command, an action which the New Yorker said "would be one of the greatest misfortunes to befall the country." He lamented to Greene that the capture of Burgoyne's army at Saratoga had bewitched the American public into "a state of perfect ease and supineness."

"Were it not that I had taken such a lead in the public politic and the sacredness of the cause we are engaged in," McDougall said, "I would not continue one moment in the service. It is truly surprising that we cannot bring our countrymen to profit neither by the experience of age nor their own. . . ."

Further word of a "plot" came from General James Varnum of Rhode Island, who was also with Washington at Valley Forge.[8] He wrote that he was "very apprehensive, as well as many others, that there is an infernal scheme forming to the prejudice of General Washington. It is conjectured that Conway's promotion is one of its blessed effects. I do not imagine that Congress are in on the plot. Possibly some of its members are."

Varnum described Valley Forge as "a place that abounds with nothing but poverty and wretchedness. Frequently our troops are destitute of provisions, and death hath fixed upon a very large number of our horses for want of forage. . . . We all feel a part of the misfortune which occasions your absence. Our sincerest wishes are for your recovery and return."

Greene reported from Valley Forge in April that "the faction seems to be dead in one form, but making its appearance in another. I am well informed there is one of your New York members [of Congress] extreme inimical to the commander-in-chief. He says it is a folly to have any considerable force, that the General [Washington] don't understand how to manage considerable bodies of men. He is a great friend to the Irish Hero [Conway]—and is closely associated with the junta. . . . Great jealousies prevail in Congress respecting the Army. They think we despise them, and are exceedingly vexed about it."[9]

With spring, however, the troubles of the winter began to disappear. Better weather and early crops made life much more pleasant at Valley Forge, and the previously absent members of Congress drifted back to their official duties. The revitalized majority then made their support of Washington clear by pulling the rug out from under the Board of War. Gates was dispatched to a command on the Hudson, where there was no doubt about his subordinate status to Washington. Conway was placed under McDougall's command, and Mifflin was chastised by Congress. Most officers refused to serve on the board, and it never regained its vitality.

It was certainly not the end to hardships in the American army, but, in many ways, the worst was over.

At that time, of course, there was no way to know that, and many worries persisted. The threat that the British would again attempt to divide the new American nation by capturing the Hudson never ceased to haunt Washington in the remaining years of the war. It was to this area that he sent McDougall, by now one of his most trusted colleagues, to guard against that dreaded possibility. Along those banks, then mostly forested and little populated, the ex-sailor was to spend much of his military career.

It was a task for which McDougall was well suited in Washington's eyes. The New Yorker was reliable, politically well connected, and a competent officer. There was an urgent need to build up the area's defenses, and Washington was confident that McDougall was up to the task. The main concern was West Point, which Washington considered the most important fort in America, and Peekskill, a village a few miles south, which was a key supply point. McDougall for many months to come would devote most of his efforts to protecting those two positions.

In March 1778, when the New Yorker returned to his home province, he learned to his horror that the command, like many across the country, was woefully deficient in men, supplies, and morale. The fortifications at West Point were little more than a collection of a few small, wooden barracks, a modest hospital, and a stone structure containing several large cannon. Washington was the first to admit how inadequate the Hudson defenses were, and he urged McDougall to build up small forts along the banks "that they may be able to resist a sudden attack of the enemy."[10]

Heading the engineering work was the brilliant Polish officer, Thaddeus Kosciusko.[11] Carefully supervising all the plans, Colonel Kosciusko pressed the effort as fast as his men were able, with enough time on the side to construct a small rock garden on the face of a cliff above the river.

McDougall also was responsible for the forging and emplacement of a huge chain designed to stretch across the river to prevent the passage of British ships. Manufactured at the Sterling Iron Works near West Point, the sixty-ton chain was securely anchored in place on April 20, 1778.[12] After that, no enemy vessel ever was able to sail north of that formidable obstacle.

South of the chain, however, the British fleet continued to menace the area from time to time. Some months earlier, when most of the defending forces had been removed to reinforce Washington at Germantown, the British captured two posts, Forts Montgomery and Clinton. Washington appointed McDougall and two other

New York in 1778, a lively city despite the British occupation. The port was busy with the constant movement of ships carrying men and supplies.

NATIONAL ARCHIVES

officers to investigate the losses.[13] The results of the court of inquiry were preordained, blaming the losses mainly on a series of blunders. The obvious fact was that the posts had been stripped by Washington's orders. The commanding officer of the forts, Brigadier General George Clinton, was also governor of New York. It would have been imprudent to make too much of the incidents, so the matter was quietly dropped.

To see if anything had been overlooked in the buildup, Washington sent Generals Greene and Knox on an inspection trip to the Hudson. On a pleasantly warm day, they arrived at Peekskill where they were greeted by McDougall and Clinton. After dinner, they sat drinking and exchanging ideas about what should be done. Later, McDougall escorted the visitors to nearby fortifications on both sides of the river. In due course, they returned to their headquarters in Morristown.

Greene reported to Washington that the chain should be protected by a boom and cables in front of it to prevent British ships from ramming it full force and a few small ships behind it which could fire at approaching enemy vessels. The officer also recommended building more batteries along the banks, and concluded that no more than 5,000 soldiers were needed to guard the highlands. In the event that the British attacked in large numbers, more Americans could be drawn from New Jersey and Connecticut.

McDougall, trying to restore his command to a semblance of order, learned that everything from clothing to beef was in short supply and his men restive. He complained to Washington that "the total derangement of almost every department at this post, occasioned by various causes, have so greatly multiplied the difficulties of the command that I have but little hopes of maintaining my reputation if the enemy should in force pay us an early visit."[14]

Even candles were hard to get, as an incident in the camp illustrated.[15] A corporal named Abner Chapman was insulted, he said, when the quartermaster offered him nothing more than a "broke and partly burnt" candle to light his quarters. Chapman angrily shouted that if he couldn't have a whole one, he wouldn't have any at all, and a fight between the two ensued.

The quartermaster, breaking loose from the assault, fled to the office of a Doctor Fanning, who headed the post hospital. Fanning sent for Chapman, who arrived a considerable time later with a stick in his hand. The physician asked the corporal why he hadn't come when summoned. Chapman answered heatedly that he simply hadn't chosen to do so. Fanning struck Chapman, who hit the doctor a return blow.

The hot-tempered corporal, found guilty by a court martial, was "reduced to a private sentinel" and lashed fifty times on his bare back.

Another of McDougall's concerns was maintaining an intelligence network in the occupied portion of the province. He was increasingly hard pressed for money, having exhausted his own fortune, and borrowed $60,000 to pay his men and buy supplies. Unlike the orderly modern system of paying for military operations from federal tax revenues, neither the provinces nor the Continental Congress was ordinarily able to raise enough money for their armies. The result was that many commanders were compelled to tap their own resources to keep things going.

Despite the problems, McDougall managed to scrape together enough money to keep his spies functioning. His agents, for example, relayed to him one of the first reports that the French had joined the war in support of the colonies—news that was greeted with elation by Washington and Congress.[16] And well they should have been elated, for French aid would prove to be the turning point in the war.

McDougall's spies also kept track of British troops entering and leaving New York, often providing first signs of a fresh offensive.

The nature of their work laid many of the spies open to suspicions about their true loyalties. Washington told McDougall on one occasion of a long interview with an agent identified only as "Mr. H." so that he would not be exposed if the letter were intercepted by the enemy.[17]

"He appears," the Virginian said, "to be a sensible man capable of rendering important service if he is sincerely disposed to do it. From what you say, I am led to hope he is. But, nevertheless, if he is really in the confidence of the enemy, as he himself believes to be the case, it will be prudent to trust him with caution and to watch his conduct with a jealous eye."

Washington added that he always considered it "necessary to be very circumspect with double spies. Their situation in a manner obliges them to trim a good deal in order to keep well with both sides, and the less they have it in their power to do us mischief the better, especially if we consider the enemy can purchase their fidelity at a higher price than we can."

Washington later had second and more troubling thoughts about "Mr. H." and a letter purportedly directed to an enemy general which the spy had intercepted and delivered to the Americans.[18] The commander-in-chief said the message probably was meant to fall into his hands, and commented: "The manner of contriving that and some other circumstances make me suspicious that he is as much in the interest of the enemy as in ours."

The administration of civilian affairs in his area also occupied a large part of McDougall's time. A particularly troublesome concern was the lawlessness that had grown in many rural regions of New York when the usual civil authorities went to war. Typical was the case of a band of army deserters who were terrorizing remote farms and villages.[19] Living in caves, they robbed and murdered citizens along the west bank of the Hudson, and also took delight in firing on small parties of American soldiers. They received money from the British, and had been offered 200 guineas by the mayor of New York City to kidnap the provincial governor. It took a substantial military operation to round them up, but eventually all were caught, tried, and condemned to death.

Another continuing problem was the movement back and forth across enemy lines of civilians with relatives and property in the occupied zone. Many travelers, probably with justification, were often suspected of spying for the other side on such trips.

On one visit, a recently widowed New Yorker, Lewis Kennedy, secured a flag of truce from McDougall to take his daughter to her grandfather in New York City.[20] Accompanied, as was the custom, by an American officer, they proceeded in a small boat downriver from Peekskill. Outside the city, they were stopped by Hessian soldiers and detained for several days in a private home.

"Every one of us," Kennedy said, "grew uneasy at being detained so long and such a disagreeable situation—no clean clothes to put on nor nothing to help pass away the time."

After dinner on Sunday, a Colonel Emmerich and a group of horsemen rode up to the house at full speed. Emmerich was "much agitated," and "asked where was the damned rebel officer."

The American escort, Captain Holden, replied: "I am the one with a flag from General McDougall."

At Emmerich's request, Holden read aloud his letter from McDougall. At that point, Kennedy said, Emmerich's "passion increased to rage and madness so that he struck Captain Holden with his fist two or three times and once with a stick."

It was extraordinary conduct for an officer, and Emmerich's associates were clearly embarrassed. One of them brought wine to the house where the Americans were taken and dismissed the guard—requesting Kennedy and Holden to remain there on their honor. Several other British officers then joined the gathering and begged the Americans to attribute the incident to Emmerich alone "and not think hard of us." At that point, the American said, "we had drank a few glasses round and got to be quite sociable."

But unknown to the group, Emmerich had entered the house and was within earshot. Kennedy said "the old colonel overheard us, upon which he came and ordered the [British] officers out of the room, saying they had no business in our company."

On the following day, several junior officers sent the Americans more wine and cherry brandy. Then Emmerich turned up and, apparently having undergone a change of heart, offered to supply the prisoners with money if they needed any. Said Kennedy: "We did not choose to be under any obligation to a man who had behaved so ungenteel." Soon afterward, they were freed and allowed to return to their lines after completing their business in the city.

As if he did not have enough problems close at hand, McDougall was ever willing to tackle national politics when the mood struck him. It did just that when Congress passed a resolution offering reconciliation to the Tories—an action that predictably raised the hackles of many of the old New York Sons of Liberty. In a fit of anger, McDougall loosed a barrage of criticism at the lawmakers, the like of which today would surely bring down the wrath of both Congress and the Pentagon.

The general called the resolution "highly unjust, injurious and dangerous to the States," adding that the crimes of the Tories were "of so heinous a nature that to let them pass with impunity would not only be unpardonable injustice to the public but make us accomplices in their guilt and draw down the wrath of Heaven upon us."[21]

McDougall was not alone in his complaints about Congress, which was again meeting in Philadelphia following evacuation of the city by the British. General Greene wrote to him that he had just spent a month in Philadelphia where he attended "the most splendid entertainments imaginable—large assemblies and evening balls." Greene complained that he was exhausted, and performed his professional duties only with great difficulty.[22]

"Our great Fabius Maximus [Washington] was the glory and admiration of the city," Greene added. "Every exertion was made to show him respect and make his time agreeable, but the exhibitions were such a scene of luxury and profusion they gave him infinitely more pain than pleasure. In a word, you never saw a degree of dissipation prevailing anywhere as now prevails in Philadelphia."

McDougall replied that he was pleased to hear about the reception for Washington, but unhappy that the capital was consumed by "dissipated manners."[23]

"It augurs ill to America," the New Yorker declared. He added that "the present manners and forms of government will not long exist together. . . . From what I experienced at the little Congress of New York, wherever a Supreme Council, such as Congress, aim to do everything, very little will be done."

Throughout the colonies, it was a time of relatively little active military campaigning. As a result, there was considerably more verbal bombast than actual bombardment of the enemy. Separated by miles of forests and rivers and often reduced by the inactivity to petty matters of administration, the Revolutionary officers had a great deal of time on their hands. They worried and complained, and did much of it by means of long, hand-written letters. McDougall was one of the most prolific authors, and some of his "favors" ran sixteen or more pages and took hours to write. He often apologized to his correspondents for being verbose, but most recipients generally did not mind. His letters provide a fascinating, firsthand exhibit of the gossip, burdens, and accomplishments of America's leaders during the years of the nation's creation.

In November 1778, McDougall, writing to Governor Clinton from a temporary assignment in Connecticut, deliberated on the whole state of affairs of the country and his situation in particular.[24]

He complained that he had been sent to Connecticut on the mistaken assumption that the British were about to attack there, and, worse, that he was so far off the beaten track that he had no decent company and had not heard from any friends.

"This is the more disagreeable," he said, "as Mrs. McDougall has been very ill at Hartford. The resignation of personal liberty is not the least sacrifice which a man makes by becoming a soldier."

McDougall noted that General Gates had been assigned to a command in Massachusetts, having chafed at being secondary to Washington on the Hudson. "And from his known temper, I suspect he prefers being the first man of a village to the second in Rome," McDougall commented. "He has but little to do there, but the service will not suffer by his being at a post of ease and security." McDougall dismissed Gates as "weak as water," and concluded that it was "fortunate for America General Burgoyne was so rash as to put himself in the position he did, and that there was no other route for him to Albany but the one he took, or he would not have been an American prisoner."

McDougall informed Clinton that the British were in the process of moving a large number of troops out of New York City. Many people, he said, concluded from this that the city was about to be evacuated. McDougall, however, advised "I cannot flatter myself that desirable event will take place soon. New York is the last post in the United States they will quit." His assessment, as it usually was on such matters, was correct.

The general observed with satisfaction that his men, mainly New Englanders, had conducted themselves admirably during the march from the Hudson to Connecticut. All too often, he said, American soldiers had looted and destroyed the property of their countrymen in such circumstances. He had tried to prevent trouble by warning the troops in advance that he would turn any transgressors over to the civil authorities for prosecution.

"The consequence has been that not a single panel of fence has been burned on the march or since we encamped," McDougall bragged. "The truth of the matter is they are much in awe of their authority and fear their reputations at home. Their countrymen would indeed conclude the devil was in them if they had conducted as they have done with the Army and in other places."

McDougall also put in a good word with the governor for his son-in-law, John Lawrance, who had been recommended for appointment as town clerk of the city of New York.

He apologized for the "wicked" nature of his request, but praised Lawrance as an industrious officer who "has preserved his morals in the Army, and the gentlemen of the law inform me who were at his examination that he made a respectable one."

He also conveyed his concern about his wife's health to Washington, and asked for permission to leave his men and visit her. The commander-in-chief gave his approval, noting in the same communication that he agreed with McDougall's advice that it would be difficult to quarter the entire army east of the Hudson.

In December 1778, McDougall wrote to Washington from Peekskill suggesting that he be allowed to remain in the highlands long enough to make the fortifications more secure along the east side of the river.[25]

"Beyond that period, I desire not to remain," McDougall declared. "Your Excellency will do me the justice to acknowledge I never sought a separate command, I never wished it. It was, and is my choice, to be with the Grand Army where there is a field for speculation and improvement . . . I was hardly recovered from a severe illness before I was honored with your commands to take charge of the highlands, disagreeable as the prospect of a separation from the Army was to me. I obeyed without a murmur, notwithstanding, then rode two miles on horseback after my disorder had seized me."

McDougall observed that he lacked enough money to pay his spies, staff to complete work assigned, and armaments to fortify the river properly. The trouble, he said, was that Congress was giving priority to other concerns and other officers.

The sensitive New Yorker complained that he was hurt because Congress repeatedly had favored others in uniform, "some of whom were unknown to the cause of this country even after the sword was drawn. . . . If I know the blots in my own character, vanity is not among those which mark it."

Continuing in a vein that would be unthinkable for most professional soldiers in the twentieth century, McDougall lamented that "it is a capricious, censorious, and perilous hour for general officers." He observed further that "I have not merited this treatment of my country. Whence it has arisen, I am at a loss to determine, unless it is that I have not meanly cringed or wickedly caballed, or that having had a halter about my neck for thirteen years for my services to America, Congress conceive themselves at liberty to treat me as they have done."

The officer also complained to Washington about the low morale in camp, and observed that he had borrowed as much as he could on his own initiative to pay for a minimum of supplies and services for the troops. Some of his men, he lamented, were "almost naked."[26]

McDougall also had alarming news about enemy spies who had acquired detailed plans of the works at West Point. Based on this and other information, the officer warned, the British seemed to be preparing for "another campaign in these states, or to attack these posts very early."

Washington, who was blessed with an abundance of patience and understanding, replied to McDougall that "you need no assurances of my perfect confidence and esteem."[27] But the commander-in-chief hinted that he was slightly annoyed by McDougall's complaints, commenting that "if you have not always been employed in the manner most agreeable to yourself, you have at least been employed."

The Virginian said he regretted "the instances you enumerate in which you have found your feelings wounded from another quarter, but you will remember, my dear sir, that we are young in the business in which we are engaged, and that more of our errors proceed from the inexperience and inadvertancy than from an inclination to do wrong."

Washington observed that "the distresses of the posts under your command for the articles of flour and forage are truly embarrassing. They are the more deplorable as similar ones are felt in every part. This camp has been reduced, not long since, to an alarming extremity for the want of forage. The truth is there is a real scarcity of the two articles. The country is in a great degree exhausted, and our money is of so little value that it affords hardly any temptation to the farmers to furnish what they have."

Nevertheless, Washington said, the commissary general had promised to send flour to McDougall as soon as possible.

One of the army's main problems was that there was not enough money entering the state and national treasuries, and therefore little to apportion—except for virtually worthless paper currency—for salaries or supplies. Many commanders, therefore, were forced to appropriate supplies from townspeople and farmers around the camps. They often received only promissory notes in return, but these had little value because it would be years before there was enough in most governmental coffers to pay any such claim. Most farmers thus became skillful at hiding their stock and grain from army search parties.

In early 1779, McDougall's aide de camp, Major Richard Platt, addressed a letter to a Peekskill Quaker, David Tuttle, "Speaker among the Friends," seeking substantial quantities of hay, oats, rye, or corn. Many Quakers were pacifists, and had declined to take part in the Revolution. Declared Platt:

> As the Friends have had an easy time of it this war by being allowed to remain peaceably on their farms and being exempted from all military duty, [they] have had nothing to do but attend to the cultivation thereof. The General directs that the above-mentioned articles be sent the first good carting sledding to his quarters at Colonel Samuel Drake's at Peekskill, and that if they are not sent in a reasonable time, he will send the bayonet among them and order all their hay and grain to be taken from them and begin with the Speaker first. Every man will be paid for his hay and grain and the transportation thereof. The Friends can proportion it among themselves in any manner they please, and the General is confident they can be under no scruple of conscience about feeding horses. . . . The General desires the Friends to remember "that they are to be subject unto the higher powers, and submit to every ordinance of man for the Lord's sake."[28]

Thus, by diplomacy or force, McDougall managed to scrape together enough supplies to survive another difficult winter in the highlands. With a sense of relief, he and his men welcomed the spring—even though it brought with it the renewed threat of another warm-weather campaign by the British. In 1779, the redcoats once again attempted to raid the American supply center at Peekskill. A fleet of ships sailed up the Hudson to a position just south of West Point, where 1,500 redcoats were landed. McDougall sent out an urgent call for help, including some of the state militia and troops from Connecticut.

"The conduct of the enemy is exceedingly inexplicable," the officer reported to Washington, "and it's extremely difficult to determine what is his object. For he has now been seven days on the river and has not made that dispatch which he might towards West Point, if that is his object. One thing, however, is very clear: that he can pillage the country without any risk."[29]

The redcoats, McDougall said, were led by Sir Henry Clinton, who had become the commander of the British army in America. It was a typical Clinton "campaign," waging small-scale skirmishes against relatively weak American positions, instead of head-on challenge. McDougall reported that Clinton "was exceeding cautious in his advance and very particular in his inquiries. He asked where I was, whether I had destroyed the bridge over Peekskill Creek, what force I had, whether the militia were alarmed, the situation of the country towards Fishkill, whether there was a great body of men at West Point, and whether your Excellency's Army was in motion this way."

Clinton managed to capture a small fort along the river, and at one time, appeared ready to move against West Point. But after several days of marching, countermarching, burning, and looting and little contact with the American forces, the austere British general pulled back his forces and retired to New York. During the remaining years of the war, there would be similar small excursions in the north, but little else. The action was beginning to take place in the South, far from McDougall's command.

Washington moved his headquarters to West Point in July 1779, and remained there until the end of the year. The garrison of the fort was placed under McDougall's direction, and during that period many of the heavy fortifications around the site were completed. Washington's forces in the area at that time totaled about 10,000, compared with 12,000 redcoats in New York.

Winter, as usual, was a time of shortages and illness in the Hudson River camps, and McDougall was not immune. He informed Washington that "a complaint of the stone which I have been afflicted with for some years is become very troublesome to me, especially in cold weather, that unless I take measure to remove it, I shall not long be able to be of much service to the country or myself."[30] He reluctantly asked for and obtained permission to leave his command in order to obtain medical care. There was little likelihood, he said, that the British would attempt "any important operations in the mid-States this winter."

He hoped to rejoin the army in a matter of weeks, but in mid-March, 1780, regretfully notified Washington from the village of Fishkill that "I find on every change from warm to cold snow weather that I am still in the same condition, and have but little expectation of being in a condition to do duty till the settled warm weather arrives."[31]

In his absence, the Hudson River commands were filled by others. On August 3, 1780, the reins at West Point were passed to Benedict Arnold, and the consequences of that action would leave scars on every officer in the American army for years to come.

In Congress at Last 10

*I*n the middle of his military career, Alexander McDougall was accorded an extraordinary opportunity—to represent his state in Congress. On October 6, 1780, the New York Legislature elected him a delegate to the Continental Congress.

"The Legislature were induced to elect you," the Assembly notified McDougall, "not only from a confidence in your abilities and integrity, but they conceived that at this juncture you would be particularly serviceable in our public councils."[1]

The lawmakers had selected him, they said, because "the preparations for the ensuing campaign will doubtless be the most important object of the deliberations of Congress during the winter." McDougall, it was thought, could "give them very useful information respecting military matters."

The legislature wanted the officer to retain his army commission, and to attend Congress "only when you conceive it can be done consistent with the duties required of you in your military capacity."

It was a fortuitous appointment in many ways. The army was increasingly restive and often at odds with Congress. The officers felt neglected, and many, including McDougall and Greene, were convinced that many delegates were more interested in drinking and carousing than in saving their country. For McDougall the election offered a welcome change of scene and opportunity to exercise his talents as a politician.

Washington also was pleased by the appointment, which he recognized as a means of getting his message—the need for more men, arms, and pay—across to Congress.

"I think your presence there at this juncture while all of the arrangements for the next campaign are before them," he told McDougall, "would be of so much utility that I cannot but take the liberty to urge your immediate compliance with the pleasure of the State. It appears to me you can in no way at this time so essentially serve the public as by going there. The moment is singularly critical, and the determination depending must have the greatest influence upon our future affairs."[2]

Thus assured, McDougall traveled twelve miles by horseback to Poughkeepsie, where the state legislature was meeting. There he buttonholed many of his old friends and former neighbors, informing them how scarcities of men and supplies were hampering the army's operations. McDougall concluded from conversations that he was elected to Congress because New York lawmakers considered "my civic capacity but a secondary one to my military."[3] He emphasized in a letter to Washington that he wanted to make sure that he would return to an army command after his service in Philadelphia, and added: "I own I fear and have much reason to fear I shall not be able in Congress to answer the virtuous expectations of the Army and my fellow citizens. But I shall endeavor to do my duty."

It was not an easy task. Many members of Congress were just as suspicious of the army as the generals were of the legislators, and the appointment of an active and politically potent officer to Congress rankled some delegates.

General Greene, who had long experience in Philadelphia, warned his friend of what lay ahead.[4] "I give you a hint," the Rhode Islander confided. "Since my arrival here, I find Congress don't approve of your taking a seat in Congress. Suppose you should write them on the subject, that you are appointed, that the commander-in-chief is desirous of your taking your seat. But as you mean to hold your commission, you wish to do nothing contrary to their views, and wish them to express their minds to you upon the subject. This will put the laboring oar upon them, and we shall see what distinctions they mean to form between the citizens and the soldiers. If it is invidious, as I am persuaded it will be, we must protest against it."

Greene had just been appointed commander of America's southern army, or what was left of it after a disastrous campaign under General Gates. Greene complained to McDougall that Congress was poor and unable to provide even enough money to get him to the South. Fortunately for America, Greene got there somehow and won national honor as one of the most skillful Revolutionary officers. But prior to the journey, he told McDougall that the command "affords but a dull prospect. The Army exists more in name than in substance. There are but a few ragged soldiers together, and those in the greatest distress imaginable, and no prospect of increasing their numbers or bettering their condition. . . ."

The tall, mercurial Rhode Islander, ever pessimistic about civilian politics, observed that "Congress are by no means alarmed at their critical condition. I think the American cause is at death's door . . . If we are saved, it must be by simplifying the government and receiving aid from the Court of France. . . ."

Such warnings might have made McDougall even more uneasy if it had not been for the fact that he had recently been in Philadelphia. There he had represented the army in presenting the protests of his fellow officers against what they considered the abuses of Congress. The whole affair was a reflection of the dissatisfaction of the soldiers and the strains between civilian and military authority. What the army mainly wanted was higher pay or assurances that salaries would be adjusted to account for inflation. A group of general officers, including McDougall, lamented that although the soldiers' grievances "have gone on increasing, no redress has been granted nor any notice been taken of their complaint."[5] The officers concluded that "the distress of the Army is great."

Discomfited by a bad horse and extremely hot weather, McDougall rode into Philadelphia in early August and asked to be heard before the full Congress. The lawmakers, however, pointed out that he would fare better if he presented his arguments first to a committee, which was duly appointed. The general told one of the Adamses that the army no longer considers that it is fighting for a republic but for people "whose object is property, and that the Army expect some of that property. . . ."[6]

McDougall noted that he had "dealt very plainly" with the Congressmen, and "this will no doubt give me a place with others in their black list." He was convinced that the majority of lawmakers wanted to do justice to the army, but that "some mean, narrow-minded souls among them artfully cast impediments in the way of doing it in a proper manner."[7] He said he would remain in Philadelphia until he had succeeded in his task "although the place is become exceedingly disagreeable to me. The heat has been and now is so intense that there is no comfort for mortals night or day." He was so busy attending meetings and presenting the army's case that he soon discovered to his mortification that old friends were complaining he had no time even to chat with them.

But his persistence paid off, for on August 12 the delegates voted to make amends to the army. The lawmakers noted that "Congress have at no time been unmindful of the military virtues which have distinguished the Army of the United States through the course of this war," and recommended adjusting pay to make up for the currency depreciation.[8] In addition, land grants were to be made to general officers, who would be awarded 1,100 acres each.

With this experience under his belt, McDougall felt relatively well equipped to take part in Congressional deliberations upon his return to Philadelphia as a full-fledged delegate. He arrived in the capital in January 1781 and discovered that one of his main tasks was to explain to the lawmakers the recent Benedict Arnold affair. Although McDougall had had nothing to do with General Arnold's defection to the British, some of the lawmakers thought the New Yorker, who commanded West Point before Arnold, might be able to explain the scandal better than other officers. But all McDougall could do was to confirm what was already common knowledge: that the brilliant, temperamental, and woman-chasing Arnold had sold out because he felt his talents had gone unrewarded by his fellow Americans. McDougall felt more bitter than most about it because Arnold, who turned over the names of many spies to the British, had crippled the New York intelligence network.

The treachery was discovered when Major John Andre, representing the British command, secretly traveled up the Hudson River to negotiate with Arnold over, among other things, the surrender of West Point. While the two men were talking on shore, American guns fired at the ship which had brought Andre, forcing it to flee without him. The two men separated and Andre, dressed in civilian clothes and posing as "John Anderson," attempted to slip back to his own lines. On the way, however, he was caught by an American patrol and, eventually, his identity discovered. The officer in charge of the patrol, Lieutenant Colonel John Jameson, immediately wrote a letter to Washington which apparently raised the first suspicions of Arnold's double-dealing.[9]

"Sir," the letter stated, "inclosed you'll receive a parcel of papers taken from certain John Anderson who has a pass signed by General Arnold as may be seen. The papers were found under the feet of his stockings. He offered the men that took him one hundred guineas and as many goods as they would please to ask. I have sent the prisoner to General Arnold. He is very desirous of the papers and everything being sent with him. But as I think they are of a very dangerous tendency . . . it more proper your Excellency should see them."

Arnold escaped to New York City, and was given the command of a British army in Virginia before departing for England. Andre, however, was tried by a military court martial and hanged. The prosecutor was Colonel John Lawrance, McDougall's English-born son-in-law, who was judge advocate general of the American army. The Jameson letter remained tucked away among the possessions of Lawrance's and McDougall's heirs until it surfaced again in 1968.

Among the incriminating papers found on Andre was a list of American spies who were supposed to be put to death immediately after capture. One so named was Captain Elijah Hunter, possibly the "Mr. H." viewed so suspiciously by Washington, who had been recommended for his job by McDougall and John Jay.[10] Hunter, despite his occupation, survived the war, and was commended for "secret services to America" by Washington.

Three months after Andre's hanging, McDougall took his seat in Congress. The shock effects of Arnold's treachery still haunted virtually every general officer in the American army. Washington, who was desperately anxious to retrieve and try Arnold, had attempted to trap the traitor and his British force in Virginia, but even with the help of a French fleet was unsuccessful. Delegate McDougall, who corresponded privately with Washington from Philadelphia under the code name, "Marcus," was asked by the commander-in-chief to propose a resolution in Congress congratulating America's new allies for their help in the effort.[11]

Washington noted in a confidential message to the New Yorker that the expedition had failed, but that the French operation "was bold and enterprising." He added that for political reasons, and "because I know it will be grateful to the French general and admiral, I take the liberty of hinting to you the propriety (if it is not already done) of Congress paying them a compliment on the occasion."

McDougall's concern about the lack of an American navy to perform tasks which the French were obliged to handle had long been an obsession with him, and became increasingly so in Congress. The ex-privateer was an ardent proponent of expanding the tiny American fleet, which had been officially created in 1775. It consisted at first of about a dozen frigates and several smaller vessels, hardly a match for the hundreds of ships commanded by the British. As a result, English sails throughout much of the war slipped unchallenged in and out of American ports, carrying reinforcements and supplies. At a time when Washington was giving some thought to the possibility of trying to retake New York City, McDougall counseled: "It is absolutely necessary to the success of our operations against New York that we have a fleet superior to the enemy, sufficient to command the navigation of the Sound, the Bay of New York, and some frigates to convoy provisions from the southard to the Army."[12]

As it was, McDougall observed, America enjoyed no such superiority, and "in this distressing condition, the hopes and expectations of our country of taking New York are very high without affording your Excellency the means of accomplishing them." For that and other reasons, the attempt was abandoned.

On February 7, 1781, a reorganization of civilian administration of America's armed forces was enacted by Congress which resulted in the creation of two new posts: Secretary of War and Secretary of

Marine.¹³ On the recommendation of Alexander Hamilton, McDougall (still a major general) was nominated and elected to the latter position. He was assigned to "oversee all naval affairs for Congress" at a salary of $5,000 a year.

The New Yorker was honored to be the first and only man to hold that job, which later became Secretary of the Navy, and declared to his fellow legislators: "If any new incentive was necessary to bind me to America or to increase my zeal for her safety and glory, this would be a powerful one. It is, however, a great satisfaction to a freeman, especially a servant of the republic, to have the approbation of its representatives."¹⁴

At the same time, he made it clear that he would not accept the job unless he could retain his army rank. He said he was convinced he could perform the duties required "without interfering with my command in the field in the active part of a campaign. I cannot, therefore, in the present critical condition of the United States in general and that of the State of New York in particular, and considering the early agency I have had in stimulating the position to the tyranny of Great Britain, think of retiring from the toils and perils of the field entirely to an office secure from danger. But if Congress think proper to leave my rank, command, pay and the future emoluments officers of my rank are entitled to for military services as they now are, I will cheerfully undertake it." He told friends he thought the job would require only six or eight months of work a year.

For a few weeks, Congress let matters stand as they were, taking no actions on McDougall's demands. The new secretary, in the meantime, set to work in the new Admiralty Office to do what he could, despite limited funds, to improve the navy. One of his most notable accomplishments was helping to put an official seal of approval on the daring exploits of his fellow Scot, Captain John Paul Jones.

Five feet five inches tall, the handsome sailor had successfully challenged the British navy on both sides of the Atlantic in ships that included an American-built sloop, *Ranger*, and a reconverted French vessel, *Bonhomme Richard*. In one of the most famous naval battles in American history, he overwhelmed the much better equipped English ship, *Serapis*, within sight of the British coast while his own vessel was ablaze and on the verge of sinking.

Jones also managed to burn British ships in their home ports, and captured many valuable cargoes. But jealousies among other commanders and Congressional misunderstanding of his exploits clouded his reputation for a time in the United States.

While McDougall was secretary, Jones arrived in Philadelphia, and the stage was set for a full-scale inquiry into the captain's exploits. A list of forty-seven questions to Jones demanded, among other things:

> When did you leave Portsmouth in New Hampshire with the *Ranger* and under what orders?
>
> What prizes did you take when you commanded her?
>
> When and by whose orders did you take command of the *Bon Homme Richard*?[15]

The draft of the inquiry concluded that "Captain Jones is required to give the fullest answers he can in writing to those questions as soon as possible. And when he has done that, the board wish[es] to have every information from him not comprised in the answers respecting his conduct since he left America." The board admonished Jones "to bring forward every light which he can on a subject which has caused so much embarrassment to the service of these States and produced inconceivable and great distress to the Army and the country. . . ."

Jones answered the questions so successfully that the board's attitude was quickly reversed.[16] The group commended the captain for having "made the Flag of America respectable among the flags of other nations." As a result of the favorable finding, Congress cleared the sailor of any implication of wrong-doing and voted "That the thanks of the United States in Congress assembled be given to Captain John Paul Jones for the zeal, prudence and intrepidity with which he hath supported the honor of the American flag. . . ."

On March 30, friends of McDougall attempted to persuade Congress to pass an act suspending the army officer's pay while serving as Secretary of Marine but allowing him to return to active military duty later.[17] The New York delegation refrained from voting, and the measure was defeated 15 to 9, with Samuel Adams of Massachusetts among those in the majority.

Instead, a motion was passed asserting "that the United States in Congress assembled have a due sense of the zeal of Major General McDougall for the safety and honor of America and applaud his magnanimity in declining 'to retire from the toils and perils of the field in the present critical condition of the United States in general and that of New York in particular.'"

The motion acknowledged that Congress was "well convinced of his wishes and dispositions to render to the public every service in his power." The delegates, however, agreed that since the general "for good reasons" wanted to remain in the army, he should vacate his office as secretary.

His long-time aide, Major Richard Platt, wrote to him from an army detachment in Newburgh, New York, commenting that "you are expected up here as soon as you have declined the appointment as Secretary of Marine. This appointment has been relished by all friends to the country with whom I have conversed. Many of them think that you have done wrong in not accepting it, but I confess I think your reasons are just."[18]

As spring greenery was appearing in Philadelphia, McDougall stepped down as secretary, bid farewell to his friends in Congress, and set out on the long ride northeast to the Hudson. He was anxious to return to what he hoped would be a more active role in winning the war.

An Embarrassing Trial 11

*W*hile the war in the North was at a standstill, the Revolution was moving toward a climax in the South.

The English generals, Clinton and Cornwallis, were blazing their way through Virginia, the Carolinas, and Georgia, overcoming virtually every major obstacle in their paths. Charleston, which had repelled a British attack early in the war, fell in 1780. Cornwallis swamped Gates at Camden, South Carolina. Nearly everywhere in the South, it seemed, the Americans were on the run.

But in late 1780 and early 1781, the war took a new direction. At King's Mountain, South Carolina, a British force sent to wipe out the pesky bands of backwoods marauders who were sniping at the redcoats from the sides was defeated by 1,500 American riflemen on horseback.

The American cause also was boosted by the arrival in December 1780 of Nathanael Greene, the vigorous New Englander who took over command of the southern department of the army. Greene was dismayed by the size and condition of his tiny, battered force of about 1,600 regulars, but was determined to make the most of it. "We have many broken bones, spilled much blood and gained but little advantage," he wrote to McDougall. "But we bear it with patience in hopes of better times. . . ."[1]

The times did, indeed, improve rapidly. Greene adopted a mobile, defensive strategy of hitting at Cornwallis when he could and pulling back when he had to do so. On a Carolina plain called Cowpens, General Daniel Morgan, although outnumbered, fought the British with such doggedness that the redcoats were soundly defeated. The vast majority of the British force, which included ex-soldiers in the American army who had joined the British after their capture at Camden, were killed or taken prisoner.

At Guilford Courthouse, North Carolina, Cornwallis outfought Greene, but lost so many men in the process that it was an empty victory. The English nobleman, short of supplies and burdened with a crippled fighting force, limped back to the port of Wilmington. Greene pushed into South Carolina, where he began to clear the countryside of many of the remaining British units.

Cornwallis viewed Greene's move to the South as a heaven-sent opportunity to take Virginia, a much richer prize than the relatively unpopulated Carolinas and Georgia. The Englishman was convinced that the battle for America could be decided in the affluent Old Dominion, and, as it turned out, he was right.

The Americans, by this time, were no longer fighting alone. The French had finally been won over by the persuasive tongue of Benjamin Franklin and others, and demonstrations at Saratoga and Germantown that the war was not a lost cause. Backing the plucky Americans, the French court decided, would be a good way to punish their arch enemies, the British. The decision proved to be the decisive factor in bringing the Revolution to a successful conclusion.

Cornwallis, obeying the orders of General Clinton, collected his forces at Yorktown on a wooded peninsula overlooking Chesapeake Bay. There he was supposed to build a strongly fortified position from which he could operate when the devastating heat of a Virginia summer gave way to cooling autumn breezes.

Washington agreed with the French general, Rochambeau, and his intrepid sailor colleague, Admiral de Grasse, that the time had come for a lightning offensive against the British at Yorktown. Pretending that he was aiming for New York City, Washington quietly steered his troops south to Virginia. After the French fleet defeated the British Navy in the Chesapeake, the way was clear to trap Cornwallis. The Englishman, with a Franco-American army in front of him and no prospect of escape to the sea, gave up on October 19. The redcoats sullenly refused to admit they had been defeated by ill-bred colonials, and tried to surrender to the French. Splendidly uniformed French officers, however, recognized the significance of the snub and directed the Englishmen to the American lines. A band played a popular tune of the day: "The World Turned Upside Down."

McDougall, who had returned to the command of West Point, received the news in a dispatch from his former aide, Major Platt, who was then serving with Washington.

"Now I have the pleasure of congratulating you on the surrender of Lord Cornwallis and the British Army," Platt declared. "Yesterday hostilities ceased and this day the enemy march out and ground their arms."[2]

The news was the cause of jubilant celebrations in the North, providing a welcome diversion from the usual boredom and apathy. In this setting petty disputes over complaints ranging from sporadic food shortages to real or imagined insults among friends often grew into serious conflicts. McDougall, writing to congratulate Washington on "the signal success of the campaign" in Virginia, noted that troops at his post had come dangerously close to mutiny over demands for more food and better quarters.[3]

The New Yorker also was disturbed by personal problems. Mrs. McDougall, the officer wrote to his son-in-law, was troubled by her eyes which "are in a very bad way, and must be exceedingly afflictive to her."[4]

Under these circumstances, the temperamental New Yorker found himself drawn into an increasingly serious quarrel with his superior, Major General William Heath. Fat and bald, the Massachusetts officer was one of the senior men in the Army, having served for many years in the militia.

The trouble began over a small purchase made by Mrs. McDougall of a few articles which were to be sent to her at camp from New York City. The items were delayed so long that she had nearly forgotten them, but eventually a merchant brought them out of the city and left them at an outlying post to be picked up by McDougall. Between the time of the purchase order and delivery, however, Washington and Heath, unknown to McDougall, banned further buying from the enemy-held city. McDougall sought permission from Heath to claim the articles, but the officer replied that only Washington or Governor Clinton could approve the request.

McDougall, observing that "the ladies often bring us into trouble," asked for and received Clinton's permission to pick up the materials.[5] It was a small incident, but enough to create an atmosphere of ill will between the two strong-minded generals.

Further troubles arose over Heath's demands on West Point for officers and enlisted men to perform various duties not directly concerned with their post. There were also disputes over the dispersion of supplies, including lumber and rum. Officers at West Point complained that they were being discriminated against while every detachment passing through the area was issued ample supplies.

Exasperated by what he considered unjust treatment, McDougall at last protested to Heath[6]: "Whatever orders you shall please to give, whether they are clearly or doubtfully in the line of service, shall be implicitly executed, . . . but permit me at the same time to inform you that it is my determination for the future to disobey every unmilitary and absurd order which may be given by any of your executive officers and to put them in arrest. . . ."

Heath regarded the statement as a clear challenge to his authority: "I do not doubt your knowledge of your own rights and the rights of those under your long and attentive military service, . . . but I must confess that some principles which seem to be hinted are to me entirely novel, both in practice and in speculation."[7]

Heath suggested that McDougall had "a right to appeal or complain to the commander-in-chief of any unmilitary practices. . . ."

The matter came to a head in the aftermath of an informal gathering at McDougall's quarters beginning in the afternoon and lasting well into the evening. Colonel Lawrance, McDougall's son-in-law who lived with the general and other members of his family, joined his father-in-law and several other officers at the table, which had been amply stocked with wine. "The glass circulated freely and the company appeared with unbent minds," Lawrance reported.[8]

As the afternoon progressed, McDougall became angrier and angrier over Heath's actions. The New Yorker recounted Heath's position just before the American evacuation of Manhattan in 1776. At a council of war at McDougall's quarters, it was recalled, Heath had advocated remaining in New York and fighting. McDougall told his subordinates that the only officers at the council who had been against the retreat were "a fool, a knave, and an obstinate honest man."[9] McDougall made it clear that General Heath, in his opinion, was the knave.

Heath, the men were told, "drew himself up into the southeast corner of the room and said that for his part he never thought New York tenable. But as so much labor and expense had been bestowed on it with Staten and Long Islands, and the country in general put so much dependence on it, he thought that a retreat would shock them too much at that period." McDougall claimed that Heath took the position "merely to gain popularity in the country."

Regarding their current quarrel, McDougall complained that Heath was deliberately bypassing him and illegally requisitioning supplies.

"Should this practice prevail," McDougall declared, "it would be in the power of an Arnold to dismantle and fell the garrison at any time. . . ."[10]

Many of the junior officers in the room agreed with McDougall—one even called Heath a coward—and urged McDougall to fight the Massachusetts veteran.[11] McDougall replied that "it was not a personal injury that was in dispute," and, besides, he was not "one of your fighting men."

Others suggested that McDougall take Heath to court. The general replied that he preferred not to trouble Washington with such an affair because the commander-in-chief "was engaged in matters of more importance to his country."

Word of the discussion soon reached Heath, who was outraged. Without hesitation, he drew up a list of seven charges against McDougall—ranging from mismanagement of supplies to "tending to lessen confidence in the commanding general"—and placed his subordinate under house arrest. McDougall remained at West Point, but the post was transferred to the command of Brigadier General John Paterson.[12]

McDougall hurriedly dispatched a letter to Washington, who was in Philadelphia: "Long ere this, I suppose, a copy of my arrest has reached you, . . . All the charges are frivolous, mean and wicked except the last [regarding McDougall's descriptions of the council of war] which alludes to a detail of simple facts. . . ."[13]

McDougall protested that Heath "has treated me like a bashaw [pasha], and has conducted to me and this post in a manner absurdly unmilitary and extremely different from that line of conduct observed by your Excellency and every other officer that hath conducted in this department . . . I beseech your Excellency to order a court martial for my trial as soon as it can possibly be arranged, for, to me, one hour of virtuous liberty is worth a whole eternity in bondage."

Washington was shocked by the dispute, which he said had made him "extremely unhappy."[14]

"Had I have had any previous notice of this disagreeable affair," he advised, "I should, as the common friend of both and for the reputation of the service, have offered my private interposition." He added that matters had gone too far for him to intervene when the dispute came to his attention.

The commander-in-chief appointed General Stirling to sit as president of the court. McDougall, however, objected to the choice, citing what he said were irregularities in a previous proceeding which Stirling had headed. As a result, the trial was postponed and another officer named as president.

McDougall promptly brought counterintelligence against Heath, including mismanagement of supplies and "unmilitary and inhuman neglect" in not erecting proper medical facilities.[15]

The trial of McDougall opened at West Point on April 17, 1782, and continued, off and on, for weeks. McDougall conducted his own defense, and presented page after page of evidence which he laboriously had collected from such sources as Washington's own log books and volumes on military law. His array of influential and friendly witnesses included the New York governor, George Clinton.

With regard to the serious charge of publicly denouncing his superior officer, McDougall claimed he was justified in describing him as a knave.

"The plain import of the word as it is then used is that he is crafty," the officer told the court. "How my repeating what passed at a council of war five years since becomes a crime, I am at a loss to conceive. It may be the interest of knaves in the cabinet and poltroons in the fields to keep the opinion delivered by members at a council of war secret, but of no others. When the object of a council of war is attained, it is not only the right but it becomes the duty of honest members to repeat them. . . ."[16]

McDougall declared that the army had been "disgraced by frequent and frivolous arrests. The controversy on which you sit in judgment is between two officers of the highest grade in the American Army. They ought after seven years service to know their duty. If I have been ignorant of mine, let your censure fall heavy on me. But if I have contended for service, contended for my own rights—rights which are essential to all officers in this Army—then I expect your censure will fall heavy, as it ought to do, on my prosecutor for a frivolous and vexatious arrest. . . ."

On August 28, the court returned its verdict. McDougall was acquitted of all charges but one: denouncing his commanding officer.[17] Some of the other charges were found to be "vexatious," and members of the court noted that McDougall had been forced to endure "embarrassments" caused by Heath's orders.

The officer's punishment was a reprimand by Washington, which the commander-in-chief complained he was issuing "with extreme reluctance." McDougall was described by Washington as an officer of high rank and "generally acknowledged merit," and was ordered back to duty as commander of a division. Washington noted that McDougall was not in the best of health, and hoped he would be able to retire briefly to his farm until he had recovered.

McDougall responded to Washington's gentle treatment by declining to counterprosecute Heath.[18] The New Yorker thought there had been too many courts martial, and said he did not want to demean further the army's reputation.

It was nearly the end of the affair, but not quite. Shortly after the finding was announced, General Stirling wrote to McDougall that "you have greatly injured me" by asking for his replacement as president of the court.[19]

"While you was under the embarrassment of a long and tedious trial by the late general court martial," Stirling explained, "I did not think it a proper time to perplex your mind by calling on you for justice." With the proceedings over, the officer added, it was time for McDougall "calmly to recollect and reflect on the injuries you have loaded me with" and render "justice" as soon as possible.

Spurning the suggestion of a duel, McDougall replied that he had, indeed, "calmly recollected," but was unable to reproach himself for his conduct.[20] "To my knowledge," McDougall said, "I have not called in question your professional character, your honor, or your integrity."

The reply did not satisfy Stirling, who retorted: "Your want of the common law on which all martial law is founded may be your misfortune, but it was highly criminal and faulty in you to sport with men's characters in the dark and under such profound ignorance . . . I could go farther and bring to your recollection by undoubted evidence a number of insinuations, whispers and dubious speeches which you have frequently thrown out with the apparent view of stabbing me in the dark. It is too low and dirty a business for me to meddle with. . . ."[21]

Stirling warned that he would spare no effort to have the "illegality" of McDougall's objections tested in court.

McDougall, exasperated, answered that "the trial is now finished and the sentence published. Does your lordship wish to have me tried again by a court martial where you are to preside? If not, it is immaterial to you, and to me, whether my exceptions to you were legal or illegal."[22]

The officer, who wanted no more of Stirling, observed that his "answers to your lordship contain no asperity or impropriety. If you expect an answer to any letter you may write in [the] future on this subject, you will please to let them be more decent than your two former ones."

A much more widespread reaction was that of McDougall's friends in Congress, who were elated by the outcome. Delegate James Duane congratulated the officer on being "rescued by the sentence of your peers from every imputation which, in the remotest degree, could reflect on your honor or your integrity. The single charge of which you are not acquitted taxes your prudence only, and not in conduct or with regard to the public, but in words respecting an individual and uttered in a social hour!"[23]

Duane concluded that "the high estimation in which your zeal . . . and your service had placed you remains unimpaired."

Faithful Guardian of His Fame   12

Although the outcome of the war was largely decided by 1782, fighting continued on a minor scale for many months, severely straining resources and tempers on both sides.

Many American commanders had been forced, for lack of funds from Congress and their home states, to dip deeply into their own pockets to maintain their regiments. General Greene, for example, found it necessary to sell his South Carolina estate in order to pay for food for his troops. He had been given the property by the state legislature in gratitude for his efforts in driving out the British.

McDougall was similarly destitute, having expended his own personal fortune in the same way.

"Although my services have not been brilliant," he observed to Governor Clinton, "yet neither the State of which I am a subject nor the Army of which I am a member have been disgraced by them. I have at no time met the enemy in the field but with more than treble my force." For his efforts, he added, "I sacrificed my ease, property, and the happiness of domestic life. For these I have refused one of the first offices of honor and profit in the gift of those States."[1]

The officer complained that he had been woefully neglected by the New York legislature, and asked for payment. The full amount he was owed, he informed General Washington, was $12,000.

"I have continued in the service under great difficulties," McDougall said, "till I am no longer able to support Mrs. McDougall at distant quarters without exposing myself to people who perhaps would rejoice at the discovery."[2] For that reason, he said, he had been forced to give up the comfortable home-in-exile where his wife had been living and transfer her to his relatively rude abode at West Point.

Illness continued to plague him, and he explained to the commander-in-chief that "a complaint of the stone" which had troubled him for four years "is very painful and distressing to me on all changes of cold weather, or when I am exposed to the cold, or in cold quarters, which unfits me for a winter's command."[3] His health also prevented him from accepting an appointment to confer with a British delegation, headed by General Carleton, about an exchange of prisoners.

With little to do except wait for an end to the Paris peace talks, the American army, which had endured enormous hardships during the war with fewer complaints than might have been expected, grew restive. Lack of pay, uncomfortable quarters, and what seemed to many an intolerable disregard for them by Congress began to rub nerves raw. Several high-ranking officers informed the commander-in-chief, "We are now reduced to a state of wretchedness."[4]

The matter was brought to a head by a group of officers from Massachusetts who asked their state to pay up. The Massachusetts lawmakers declined to do so, and suggested that the officers take their troubles to Congress. The situation grew increasingly serious, with some soldiers hinting at mutiny and officers proposing they all resign en masse. Washington was so alarmed he decided not to return to Mount Vernon for the winter, but remained with the main body of troops at West Point and nearby Newburgh.[5] The hotheads were at least temporarily talked out of their rebellion by officers such as Washington who proposed instead that a list of grievances be drawn up and presented to Congress. For the second time, the army chose McDougall to head a delegation to Philadelphia, assisted by Colonels John Brooks and Matthias Ogden. One

Faithful Guardian of His Fame

of the group's most important suggestions was an offer by the army to settle for a flat sum instead of the half wartime pay for life the soldiers had been promised earlier. Demands also included assurance that enlisted men would be paid an $80 bonus they were owed.

McDougall, who had recovered from his fevers, accepted the assignment, but had to ask another officer to lend him an aide to ride with him to the capital. "I am destitute of a proper waiter to accompany me to Philadelphia," he explained. "Some of those allowed me and the family are sick, and all are too raged for that service."[6]

By the time the officer arrived in Philadelphia, the American and British negotiators had reached an agreement on the peace settlement, and hostilities between the two countries ceased. Some of the soldiers began to head homeward, but many stayed on awaiting the outcome of the conferences in Philadelphia. There was a widespread feeling that if they didn't stick together now, they would never be rewarded for their long years of fighting.

The memorial McDougall presented to Congress was an eloquent summary of the Army's case. The officers complained that they had fought on despite their sufferings, but that their patience was wearing thin as their problems multiplied.

The memorial stated:

> We have borne all that men can bear—our property is expended—our private resources are at an end, and our friends are wearied out and disgusted with our incessant applications. We, therefore, most seriously and earnestly beg that a supply of money may be forwarded to the Army as soon as possible. The uneasiness of the soldiers, for want of pay, is great and dangerous. Any further experiments on their patience may have fatal effects.[7]

Many members of Congress believed that the soldiers' demands were justified. But there was simply not enough money flowing into the tax coffers to pay the men all they wanted. American credit was overdrawn in Europe, and some civilian officials also were deeply in debt for having expended their own accounts and borrowed from others to help keep the wartorn country operating.

Thoroughly embarrassed by the dilemma, a Virginia delegate said he wished the army's memorial "could with propriety be promulgated throughout the United States. They would, I am sure, at least put to shame all those who have labored to throw a fallacious gloss over our public affairs."

A Congressional committee assembled on the evening of January 13, 1783, to listen to McDougall, Brooks, and Ogden.[8] James Madison, who later became the fourth President of the United States, described the trio as painting "their suffering and services, their successive hopes and disappointments throughout the whole war in very high-colored expressions, and signified that if a disappointment were now repeated, the most serious consequences were to be apprehended."

McDougall told the committee that the army was "verging to that state which we are told will make a wise man mad."[9] At the same time, he observed that many soldiers were sympathetic to the problems confronting Congress because of "the debility and defects in the Federal Government, and the unwillingness of the States to cement and invigorate it." The officer said that if Congress were dissolved, it would reduce the benefits gained from the war and that rivalry among the states would result.

Colonel Ogden said he did not want to return to the army if he had to bring bad news. Colonel Brooks warned that the soldiers were so upset that they did not always reason coolly, and that "a disappointment might throw them blindly into extremities."

The issue was complicated by attempts of some members of Congress, such as Alexander Hamilton, to enmesh the delegation in a dispute between the federalists and those favoring strong states' rights. The federalists perceived that the army's complaints could be used to strengthen the case for a strong central government, especially if there was a threat of mutiny hovering in the background.

McDougall was apprised of the arguments, and wrote to General Knox: ". . . What if it should be proposed to unite the influence of Congress with that of the Army and the public creditors to obtain permanent funds for the United States which will promise most ultimate security for the Army?"[10]

After several weeks of negotiation, the deputation was able to make only a little headway with their demands. The lawmakers

Faithful Guardian of His Fame 151

continued to declare that there simply was no money to comply with the requests.

"A month's pay in notes to the officers and one to the non coms and privates at weekly payments of half dollar per week to the latter is all that can now be obtained," McDougall wrote to Knox, who was with the army at West Point.[11]

Knox began to despair that the matter ever would be settled, observing to McDougall: "Posterity will hardly believe that an Army contended incessantly for eight years under a pressure of misery to establish the liberties of their country without knowing who were to compensate them or whether they were even to receive any reward for their services. . . ."[12]

Knox observed that "there is a point beyond which there is no sufferance. I pray sincerely we may not pass it."

Not long afterward, Knox informed McDougall that the officers again were growing restless as a result of the impasse in Philadelphia. Knox said that "papers, unknown by whom, have been circulated through the cantonment requesting all the general and field officers and an officer from each company to meet . . ." but that a postponement had been requested by Washington.[13] "This is certain: The officers' expectations are at an end, and that they wish to do something to obtain that justice which has hitherto from a variety of causes been denied them. . . . What will be the consequences, God knows. I sincerely hope we shall not be influenced to actions which may be contrary to our uniform services of eight years. The men who by their illiberality and injustice drive the Army to the very brink of destruction ought to be punished with severity."

Knox ended with this advice: "Endeavor, my dear friend, once more to convince the obdurate of the awful evils which may arise from postponing a decision upon the subjects of our address."

Many scholars believe the time was ripe for mutiny, and that Washington, had he been of a different frame of mind, might have used the army to establish a military dictatorship. But that was not the Virginian's way, and he called his officers together on March 15 at Newburgh to hear the report of the McDougall committee.

Finding it difficult to speak, he falteringly began to read from a prepared statement—and then drew his eyeglasses from a pocket: "Gentlemen, you will permit me to put on my spectacles, for I have not only grown gray, but almost blind, in the service of my country."[14] Many of the officers were moved to tears, and, if they had previously been inclined to mutiny, were swayed by Washington's address, a copy of which was sent to Philadelphia for McDougall's perusal.

Washington admonished the anonymous writer of the tract against his suggestion that the army retire into the wilderness and let an "ungrateful country" defend itself.

"But who are they to defend?" the commander-in-chief demanded. "Our wives, children, our farms, and other property which we leave behind us?"[15]

Washington noted that the writer had advised the army against sheathing its swords until the claims were settled, and declared:

> This dreadful alternative of either deserting our country in the extremest hour of her distress or turning our arms against it (which is the apparent object, unless Congress can be compelled into an instant compliance) has something shocking in it that humanity revolts at the idea. My God! What can this writer have in view by recommending such a measure?. . . . A moment's reflection will convince every dispassionate mind of the physical impossibility of carrying either proposal into execution.[16]

Following the address, the officers quickly responded by passing a resolution, proposed by Knox, "that the Army continue to have unshaken confidence in the justice of Congress and their country" and refuting "with abhorrence" the anonymous tract. The officers also expressed their thanks to McDougall for his work in Philadelphia, and requested him "to continue his solicitations at Congress until the objects of his mission are accomplished."[17]

Congress, at last, approved full pay for officers for five years, with full pay for four months for enlisted men. Arrangements for actual payment were not immediately settled, and the matter was not finally put to rest for many years, long after many of the veterans were dead. For the moment, however, the action was widely interpreted by the army as a vote of confidence in them. There was little talk thereafter of mutiny among the regular soldiers, although a rebellious party briefly went on a rampage in Philadelphia in June.

Some of the lawmakers, however, were still suspicious of the army's intentions, and were further dismayed by the formation on May 13 of the Society of the Cincinnati. The organization, instigated by General Knox and several of his friends, was intended to be a permanent association of the Revolutionary officer corps and their descendants. The group was formally installed at the headquarters of General Friedrich von Steuben.[18] Washington was elected president-general and McDougall treasurer-general. The society declared itself to be a social body, and members made it clear they were not interested in using the group for political purposes.

McDougall, nevertheless, was still very much interested in reestablishing himself as a political leader. He was frustrated by the prolonged British occupation of New York City, to which he was eager to return. Even though the war was officially over, the British kept possession of New York City until late November 1783. It was a much less imposing community than it had been before the war. McDougall observed that two-fifths of the city's houses, which numbered 5,000 before the conflict, had been burned or destroyed by other means. Two-fifths of the residents were refugees.

On the outskirts of town and in some sections of the inner city, masses of shanties and tents had been erected to house the thousands of soldiers who otherwise might have found comfortable lodging in homes that had existed before the war. Cut off by the victorious American army from their usual farm sources of food, the remaining inhabitants paid many times more than normal prices for what little did get through the lines or was imported. Many churches were in use as military offices or storehouses.

The traditional glitter of New York society had long since dimmed as the British withdrew their forces. The harbor was jammed with ships laden with departing soldiers and civilian loyalists. The Tories, many of whom were heading for lands reserved for them in Canada, sold as many of their possessions as they could. Valuable cabinets, clocks, and pictures were bargained away for next to nothing. The streets were filled with American ex-prisoners, many of whom had spent years of confinement aboard rotting jail ships off Manhattan. Some of the soldiers, although happy to be free again, were despondent about the apathy with which they were greeted by their fellow citizens. In a mood often echoed over the years by other veterans,

Elijah Fisher, released from one of the prison ships, wrote after a week in New York:

> I come down by the market and sits down all alone, almost discouraged, and begun to think over how that I had been in the Army, what ill success I had met with there and also how I was wronged by them I worked for at home, and lost all last winter, and now that I could not get into any business and no home, which you may well think how I felt. But then come into my mind that there were thousands in worse circumstances than I was, and having food and raiment [I should] be content, and that I had nothing to reflect on myself, and I [resolved] to do my endeavor and leave the event to Providence, and after that I felt as contented as need be.[19]

While all this was going on prior to the official evacuation, McDougall was itching to return to the city from which most American officers still were barred.

More than a month before evacuation of the last redcoats, the officer asked Washington for permission to visit the community and look after two estates for which he was executor. One of the properties, he explained, had declined in value because he was not able to enter the city and sell it while prices were high.[20] He said he was "deterred from availing myself of that favorable opportunity to make sale of the houses in hopes the British would long ere this have left the city and to avoid setting a bad example. But their stay has lengthened out far beyond my expectation."

Prior to the evacuation, some of the hottest-headed "patriots," who wanted revenge for their suffering during the war, planned to plunder New York when the British left. Three or four hundred men were reported to be ready to sack the city if they had but half a chance. They sought help from McDougall, but he turned them down. As a result, one member of the group accused the officer of having made a deal with the Tories who had remained in the city — a charge he subsequently took back with an apology.[21]

The long-awaited evacuation took place on November 25. The British troops marched out of the heart of the city, and began board-

Faithful Guardian of His Fame 155

ing ships in the harbor. Before all of them had left, the American columns started marching in, led by Washington and Governor Clinton.

A crowd gathered as the column proceeded into Fort George. There the soldiers were incensed to find that an embittered redcoat had nailed the Union Jack to the top of a post, removed the apparatus for pulling it down, and, for good measure, greased the pole. An American seaman saved the day by donning nailed boots and shinnying up the pole, where he removed the British flag and replaced it with the Stars and Stripes. The last British soldiers rowed silently to their ships as American guns roared a salute to the new nation.

At noon on December 4, more than forty of Washington's top officers, including Generals Greene, Knox, von Steuben, Gates, Kosciusko, Hamilton, and McDougall, gathered at Fraunces' Tavern for a farewell to the commander-in-chief.[22] In a long, handsome room on the second floor, tables were laden with food and wine, and there the splendidly uniformed officers waited nervously. When Washington entered the room, emotions were "too strong to be concealed" and a silence fell as the commander-in-chief prepared to deliver his parting address.

Washington filled his glass with wine, turned to the men, and said: "With a heart full of love and gratitude, I now take leave of you. I most devoutly wish that your latter days may be as prosperous and happy as your former ones have been glorious and honorable."

General Knox was closest to Washington, and he turned silently and embraced the commander. Tears in their eyes, every officer in the room marched up to Washington and kissed him. It was too highly charged a scene to last long, and Washington departed quickly, accompanied by his friends to a nearby boat in which he started the trip home to Mount Vernon.

It was time to begin rebuilding, and McDougall pitched into the effort with characteristic vigor despite recurring bad health, a legacy of the war. He once again was elected to various political posts, including the New York Senate where he served from 1784 to 1786. He was active in efforts to keep the state on a "hard-money" basis, against repeated attempts to augment metal coins with paper money. McDougall also backed legislation to separate church from state, reflecting the pre-war struggles of his fellow Presbyterians against the tax-supported Anglican Church.

In New York City, he was also active, along with other prominent citizens, in reestablishing the city's commerce. He helped to organize the state's first bank, the Bank of New York, and was elected its first president.[23] Among its directors was Alexander Hamilton, who was making his influence felt in many aspects of the nation's finances. McDougall declined reelection to the bank's presidency after a short term in office, and plunged instead into what he considered more personally rewarding ventures.

Attempting to revive his old business contacts with the West Indies, he informed a friend from Grenada that "I have several important propositions in commerce and finance to make prudent, close-mouthed gentlemen in the islands. . . . I am at the head of all political and commercial information, Continental and State. I left the chair of the bank because it was too confined a life to me."[24] He added that he was "still a stockholder and depositor for a considerable sum," and invited the gentleman to "a family Presbyterian dinner with us at half past 2 o'clock."

As the patriarch of his clan in the state, he also was responsible for many matters of a personal nature. In this capacity, he asked a kinsman in Argyle, New York (the community which had been only in the planning stages when he arrived in America a half century earlier) to find quarters for his "natural sister," Eleanor Leach.

"In her lifetime," McDougall said, "she has been very industrious. She is now grown old and little able to provide for herself. To maintain her in this city would cost me more than I can spare from the great arrearage due to me from the public. I have therefore cast my eye on Argyle as a proper place for her, where she can be boarded reasonably."[25]

In early 1786, McDougall's health declined rapidly. He continued to take part in Senate sessions, and renewed his opposition to paper money. By April, he was confined to bed for a time, but was carried on a stretcher into the Senate for a crucial vote against legalizing "soft currency." Moments later, he left the chamber and never returned. On June 10, 1786, at the age of fifty-three, he died at his

Faithful Guardian of His Fame

home on Nassau Street in New York and was buried in the Old Presbyterian Church yard.[26] Members of Congress, military officers, foreign ambassadors, and throngs of New Yorkers marched in a procession to the church as guns fired a final salute.

The *New York Gazetteer* paid tribute to him as a man "distinguished by many conspicuous proofs of an ardent and pure attachment to the principles of liberty. The memorable stand he made in support of the freedom of the press will not be easily forgotten. And the part he acted in the revolution has finished his claim to the illustrious character of patriot.

> He espoused the cause of American liberty in adversity, and was constant to her in all the vicissitudes of her fortune. At the earliest period of the contest, he stood foremost a mark for the indignation of offended power, and in the progress of that contest was ever ready in the field or Senate to brave its utmost resentment.
>
> Of strong intellect, prudent and sagacious in council, of deliberate courage in the field, he had equal claims as a soldier or statesman. . . . While integrity, love of country, fortitude and abilities continue to be esteemed, this sentiment will be the faithful guardian of his fame.[27]

Appendix

"To the Betrayed Inhabitants of the City and Colony of New York," December 16, 1769.

In a day when the minions of tyranny and despotism in the mother country and the colonies, are indefatigable in laying every snare that their malevolent and corrupt hearts can suggest, to enslave a free people when this unfortunate country has been striving under many disadvantages for three years past, to preserve their freedom; which to an Englishman is as dear as his life,—when the merchants of this city and the capital towns on the continent, have nobly and cheerfully sacrificed their private interest to the public good, rather than to promote the designs of the enemies of our happy constitution: It might justly be expected, that in this day of constitutional light, the representatives of this colony would not be so hardy, nor be so lost to all sense of duty to their constituents, (especially after the laudable example of the colonies of Massachusetts Bay and South Carolina before them) as to betray the trust committed to them. This they have done in passing the vote to give the troops a thousand pounds out of any monies that may be in the Treasury, and another thousand out of the money that may be issued, to be put out on loan, which the Colony will be obliged to make good, whether the Bill for that purpose does or does not obtain the Royal assent; and that they have betrayed the liberties of the people, will appear from the following consideration; to wit; that the Ministry are waiting to see whether the Colonies, under their distressed circumstances, will divide on any of the grand points which they are united in, and contending for, with the mother country; by which they may carry their designs against the Colonies, and keep in Administration.

For if this should not take place, the Acts must be repealed, which will be a reflection on their conduct, and will bring the reproach and clamor of the nation on them, for the loss of trade to the empire, which their malconduct has occasioned.

Our granting money to the troops, is implicitly acknowledging the authority that enacted the Revenue Acts, and their being obligatory on us, as these Acts were enacted for the express purpose of taking money out of our pockets without our consent; and to provide for the defending and support of Government in America; which revenue we say by our grant of money, is not sufficient for the purpose aforesaid; therefore we supply the deficiency.

This was the point of view in which these Acts were considered, by the Massachusetts and South Carolina Assemblies, and, to prevent that dangerous construction, refuted it. On this important point, we have differed with these spirited Colonies, and do implicitly approve of all the tyrannical conduct of the Ministry to the Bostonians, and by implication censure their laudable and patriotic denial. For if they did right (which every sensible American thinks they did) in refusing to pay the billeting money, surely we have done wrong, very wrong, in giving it. But our Assembly says that they do their duty in granting money to the troops: Consequently, the Massachusetts Assembly did not do theirs, in not obeying the Ministerial mandate. If this is not a division in this grand point, I know not what is: And I doubt not but the Ministry will let us know it is to our cost, for it will furnish them with arguments and fresh courage.

Is this a grateful retaliation to that brave and sensible people, for the spirited and early notice they took of the suspending Act? No, it is base ingratitude, and betraying the common cause of liberty.

To what other influence than the deserting the American cause, can the Ministry attribute so pusilanimous a conduct as this is of the Assembly; so repugnant and subversive of all the means we have used, and opposition that has been made by this and the other colonies, to the tyrannical conduct of the British Parliament! To no other. Can there be a more ridiculous farce to impose on the people than for the Assembly to vote their thanks to be given to the merchants, for entering into an agreement not to import goods from Britain, until the Revenue Acts should be repealed, while they at the same time counteract it by countenancing British acts, and complying with ministerial requisitions, incompatible with our freedom? Surely they cannot.

And what makes the Assembly's granting this money the more grievous is, that it goes to the support of troops kept here not to protect but to enslave us: Has not the truth of this remark been lately exemplified in the audacious, domineering and inhuman Major Pullaine, who ordered a guard to protect a sordid miscreant, that transgressed the laudable nonimportation agreement of the merchants, in order to break that, which is the only means left them, under God, to baffle the designs of their enemies to enslave this Continent? This consideration alone ought to be sufficient to induce a free people not to grant the troops any supply whatsoever, if we had no dispute with the mother country, that made it necessary not to concede anything that might destroy our freedom; reasons of economy and good policy suggest that we ought not to grant the troops money.

Whoever is the least acquainted with the English history, must know, that grants frequently made to the crown, is not to be refused, but with some degree of danger of disturbing the repose of the Kingdom or Colony. This evinces the expediency of our stopping these grants now while we are embroiled with the mother country, that so we may not, after the grand controversy is settled, have a new bone of contention about the billeting money; which must be the case if we do not put an end to it at this time: for the Colony, in its impoverished state, cannot support a charge which amounts to near as much per annum, as all the other expenses of the government besides.

Hence it follows that the assembly have not been attentive to the liberties of the Continent, nor to the property of the good people of this Colony in particular, we must therefore attribute this sacrifice of the public interest, to some corrupt source. This is very manifest in the guilt and confusion that covered the faces of the perfidious abettors of this measure, when the house was in debate on the subject. Mr. Colden knows from the nature of things, that he cannot have the least prospect to be in administration again; and therefore, that he may make hay while the sun shines and get a full salary from the Assembly, flatters the ignorant members of it, with the consideration of the success of a bill to emit a paper currency; when he and his artful coadjutors must know, that it is only a snare to impose on the simple; for it will not obtain the Royal assent. But while he is solicitous to obtain his salary, he must attend to his posterity, and as some of his children hold offices under the government, if he did not procure an obedience to his requisition, or do his duty in case the Assembly refused the billeting money, by dissolving them, his children might be in danger of losing their offices. If he dissolved the Assembly, they would not give him his salary.

The De Lanc[e]y family knowing the ascendancy they have in the present house of Assembly, and how useful that influence will be to their ambitious designs, to manage a new governor, have left no stone unturned to prevent a dissolution. The Assembly, conscious to themselves, of having trampled on the liberties of the people, and fearing their just resentments on such an event, are equally careful to preserve their seats, expecting that if they can do it at this critical juncture, as it is imagined the grand controversy will be settled this winter, they will serve for seven years; in which time they hope the people will forget the present injuries done to them. To secure these several objects, the De Lanc[e]y family, like true politicians, although they were to all appearance at mortal odds with Mr. Colden, and represented him in all companies as an enemy to his country, yet a coalition is now formed in order to secure to them the sovereign lordship of this Colony. The effect of which has given birth to the abominable vote, by which the liberties of the people are betrayed. In short, they have brought matters to such a pass, that all the checks resulting from the form of our happy constitution are destroyed. The Assembly might as well invite the council to save the trouble of formalities, to take their seats in the house of Assembly, and place the Lieut. Governor in the Speaker's chair, and then there would be no wast[e] of time in going from house to house, and his honor would have the pleasure to see how zealous his former enemies are in promoting his interest to serve themselves. Is this a state to be rested in, when our all is at a stake? No, my countrymen, rouse! Imitate the noble example of the friends of liberty in England, who, rather than be enslaved, contend for their right with k--g, lords and commons. And will you suffer your liberties to be torn from you, by your representatives? Tell it not in Boston; publish it not in the streets of Charles-Town! You have means yet left to preserve a unanimity with the brave Bostonians and Carolinians; and to prevent the accomplishment of the designs of tyrants. The house was so nearly divided, on the subject of granting the money in the way the vote passed, that one would have prevented it; you have, therefore, a respectable minority. What I would advise to be done is, to assemble in the fields, on Monday next, where your sense ought to be taken on this important point; notwithstanding the impudence of Mr. Jauncey, in his declaring to the house that he had consulted his constituents, and that they were for giving money. After this is done, go in a body to your members, and insist on their joining with the minority to oppose the bill; if they dare refuse your just requisition, appoint a committee to draw up a state of the whole matter, and send it to the speakers of the several houses of assembly on the Continent, and to the friends of our cause in England, and publish it in the newspapers, that the whole world may know your sentiments on this matter, in the only way your circumstance will admit. And I am confident it will spirit the friends of our cause and chagrin our enemies. Let the notification to call the people be so expressed that whoever absents himself, will be considered as agreeing to what may be done by such as shall meet—and that you may succeed, is the unfeigned desire of

                              A SON OF LIBERTY

Notes

Preface

1. R. W. Griswold, *Washington and the Generals of the American Revolution* (Philadelphia: Lippincott, 1866).
2. Letter, Lieutenant Colonel Gauvion, April 1, 1799, Alexander McDougall Papers, New-York Historical Society (hereafter cited as NYHS).
3. Wilbur C. Abbott, *New York in the American Revolution* (New York: Charles Scribner's Sons, 1929).
4. Thomas Jones, *History of New York During the Revolutionary War*, Edward F. DeLancey, ed. (New York: NYHS, 1879).
5. Jared Sparks, Letter, July 18, 1832, W. Wright Hawkes Collection, Union College, Schenectady, N. Y.

Chapter One

1. "The Letters and Papers of Cadwallader Colden," New-York Historical Society (hereafter cited as NYHS) *Quarterly,* 1921, Vol. V, p. 284. (Note: In many cases, spelling and punctuation have been modernized in this book.)

2. J. P. MacLean, *An Historical Account of the Settlements of Scotch Highlanders in America Prior to the Peace of 1783* (Baltimore: Geneological Publishing Co., 1968), p. 176.

3. J. McVicar, minister, Letter, Torrodale in the Isle of Islay, Scotland, 1738, Alexander McDougall Papers (hereafter cited as M papers), NYHS.

4. Baptismal Register, Kildalton Parish, Islay, Scotland, September 7, 1732, June 19, 1735, December 26, 1737.

5. Jones, *History of New York During the Revolutionary War,* Vol. I, p. 25.

6. Susan Lyman, *The Story of New York* (New York, 1964).

7. Records, Isle of Islay, Scotland.

8. Moncreiffe of That Ilk and David Hicks, *The Highland Clans* (London: Barrie & Rockliff, 1967), inside cover.

9. "Memoirs and a Journal of the Presbyterian Congregation in the City of New York," First Presbyterian Church, New York.

10. Anson Phelps Stokes and Leo Pfeffer, *Church and State in the United States* (New York, 1964), p. 21, indicates how the divergence of churches in America also helped to foster divergence in politics.

11. *Pennsylvania Journal,* March 22, 1770.

12. Robert Emmet Wall, Jr., "Louisbourg, 1745," *New England Quarterly* Vol. XXXII, No. 1 (March 1964), describes difficulties in capturing the fort.

13. William B. Clark, ed., *Naval Documents of the American Revolution,* Alexander McDougall (hereafter cited as M) to John Jay, December 24, 1775, (Washington, D.C.: U. S. Government Printing Office, 1964), Vol. III, p. 225.

14. Document, Torrodale, Isle of Islay, Scotland, 1751, M Papers, NYHS.

15. Stephen McDougall to M, March 19, 1752, M Papers, NYHS.

16. Stephen McDougall to Nancy McDougall, 1752, M Papers, NYHS.

17. Shipping list of *Tyger,* 1757, M Papers, NYHS.

18. Stuyvesant Fish, *The New York Privateers, 1756-1763* (New York: George Graly Press, 1945).

19. *New York Gazette,* October 3, 1757.

20. *New York Mercury,* February 20, 1758.

21. *New York Mercury,* October 17, 1757.

22. *New York Mercury,* November 7, 1757.

23. *New York Mercury,* May 15, 1758.

24. Stephen McDougall to M, August 29, 1758, M Papers, NYHS.

25. Letter of marque, 1759, M Papers, NYHS.

26. *New York Mercury,* July 9, 1759.

27. Jones, *History of New York During the Revolutionary War,* Vol. I.

28. "To the Publick," 1777, M Papers, NYHS.

Chapter Two

1. Carl Bridenbaugh, *Cities in Revolt* (New York: Alfred A. Knopf, 1955).
2. Waste-Book, W. Wright Hawkes Collection, Union College, Schenectady, N. Y.
3. Stephen McDougall to M, September 4, 1766, Hawkes Collection, Union College.
4. M to Rachel McDougall, August, 1764, M Papers, NYHS.
5. Stephen McDougall to M, September 4, 1766, M Papers, NYHS.
6. Waste-Book, Hawkes Collection, Union College, and *General Catalogue of Princeton University, 1746-1906*, Princeton University, 1908.
7. Waste-Book, Hawkes Collection, Union College.
8. Waste-Book, Hawkes Collection, Union College.
9. Stephen McDougall to M, September 4, 1766, M Papers, NYHS.
10. Wilbur C. Abbott, *New York in the American Revolution*, (New York: Charles Scribner's Sons, 1929), p. 55.
11. Ibid., p. 33.
12. Pauline Maier, *From Resistance to Revolution*, (New York: Vintage Books, 1974) (orig. New York: Knopf, 1972).
13. "To the Free and Loyal Inhabitants of the City and Colony of New York," May 1770, Hawkes Collection, Union College.
14. L. Jesse Lemisch, "New York's Petitions and Resolves of December, 1765: Liberals vs. Radicals," NYHS *Quarterly* Vol. XLIX, No. 4, (October 1965), shows how respectable liberal professionals became involved in anti-British agitation.
15. "To the Betrayed Inhabitants of the City and Colony of New York," broadsheet, December 1769, New York Public Library.
16. Jones, *History of New York During the Revolutionary War*, p. 426.
17. E. B. O'Callaghan, ed., *The Documentary History of the State of New York* (Albany, N.Y.: 1850), Vol. III, p. 317.

Chapter Three

1. Abbott, *New York in the American Revolution*, p. 84.
2. "Public Papers of George Clinton," State of New York, 1899, Vol. I, p. 49.
3. Ibid.

4. Ibid.

5. Pauline Maier, "Popular Uprisings and Civil Authority in Eighteenth Century America," *William and Mary Quarterly*, Third series, Vol. XXVII, No. 1 (January 1970), describes the ferment in New York and other colonies in the colonial period.

6. "To the Freeholders, Freemen and Inhabitants of the County of New York, and to all the Friends of Liberty in North America," written by M, *Boston Gazette*, February 26, 1770.

7. Letter to public by M, *New York Journal*, February 24, 1770.

8. An excellent biography of Wilkes is Audrey Williamson's *Wilkes: A Friend to Liberty* (New York: Reader's Digest Press/E. P. Dutton, 1974).

9. *New York Journal*, March 29, 1770.

10. Ibid.

11. Colden's dispatch to Lord Hillsborough, February 21, 1770, in Jones, *History of New York During the Revolutionary War*, p. 431.

12. A. P. Stokes, I. N. Phelps, ed., *The Iconography of Manhattan Island* (New York, 1915-1928), Vol. 3, appendix plate 4b.

13. *New York Journal*, April 19, 1770.

14. *New York Gazette*, April 9, 1770.

15. *New York Journal*, April 19, 1770.

16. *Boston Gazette*, February 26, 1770.

17. *Pennsylvania Journal*, March 22, 1770.

18. John C. Miller, *Origins of the American Revolution* (Boston: Little, Brown, 1943), p. 305.

19. Jones, *History of New York During the Revolutionary War*, Vol. I, p. 29.

20. Substance of the evidence against Captain McDougal (sic), M Papers, 1770, NYHS.

21. *New York Journal*, May 3, 1770.

22. Jones, *History of New York During the Revolutionary War*, Vol. I, p. 32.

23. "To the Freeholders and Freemen of the City and Colony of New York," by M, December 22, 1770; "To the Freeholders and Freemen of the City and Colony of New York, and to all the Friends of Liberty in the British Empire," by M, January 26, 1771, NYHS.

24. Lynton K. Caldwell, "George Clinton—Democratic Administrator," *New York History* Vol. XXXII, No. 1 (January 1951), describes Clinton's thirty years of service to New York.

25. "To the Freeholders and Freemen of the City and Colony of New York," December 22, 1770; "To the Freeholders and Freemen of the City and Colony of New York, and to all the Friends of Liberty in the British Empire," January 26, 1771.

26. Michael G. Kammen, "The Colonial Agents, English Politics, and the American Revolution," *William and Mary Quarterly,* Third series, Vol. XXII, No. 2 (April 1965), describes the difficulties of lobbying in London.

27. Benjamin Franklin to M, March 18, 1770, Hawkes Collection, Union College.

Chapter Four

1. *New York Journal,* June 7, 1770.
2. Miller, *Origins of the American Revolution,* p. 310.
3. "To the Free and Loyal Inhabitants of the City and Colony of New York," May 16, 1770, Hawkes Collection, Union College.
4. Merrill Jensen, *The Founding of a Nation: A History of the American Revolution, 1763-1776* (New York: Oxford, 1968), p. 365.
5. Abbott, *New York in the American Revolution,* p. 95.
6. Bernard Mason, *The Road to Independence, the Revolutionary Movement in New York, 1773-1777* (Lexington, Ky., 1966).
7. Miller, *Origins of the American Revolution,* p. 311.
8. Ibid., p. 325. Chapter 11 of Miller's book details the extent of the calm and its effects in America and England.
9. Boston Committee of Correspondence Manuscripts, December 13, 1773.
10. M papers, May 12, 1774, NYHS.
11. M Papers, May 13, 1774, NYHS.
12. M Papers, May 14, 1774, NYHS.
13. Miller, *Origins of the American Revolution,* p. 363.
14. M Papers, May 16, 1774, NYHS.
15. Ibid.
16. Ibid.
17. Jensen, *The Founding of a Nation: A History of the American Revolution, 1763-1776,* p. 472.
18. M Papers, May 17, 1774, NYHS.
19. Abbott, *New York in the American Revolution,* p. 106.
20. Ibid.
21. Ibid., p. 109.
22. M Papers, May 24, 1774, NYHS.
23. M to Charles Thomson, June 1, 1774, NYHS.
24. M and Isaac Sears to Samuel Adams, June 20, 1774, M Papers, NYHS.

Chapter Five

1. "Public Papers of George Clinton," State of New York, Vol. I, p. 69.
2. Abbott, *New York in the American Revolution*, p. 115.
3. Jensen, *The Founding of a Nation: A History of the American Revolution, 1763-1776*, p. 481.
4. Ibid.
5. Jones, *History of New York During the Revolutionary War*, p. 449.
6. Ibid.
7. Ibid., p. 451.
8. Broadus Mitchell, *Alexander Hamilton: Youth to Maturity*, (New York: Macmillan, 1957), p. 63.
9. Alexander Hamilton to M, probably 1775, Hawkes Collection, Union College.
10. Jones, *History of New York During the Revolutionary War*, p. 456.
11. Samuel Eliot Morison, *The Oxford History of the American People*, Vol. I, (New York: Oxford, 1965), Chapter XIV.
12. Miller, *Origins of the American Revolution*, p. 380.
13. Richard B. Morris, *Encyclopedia of American History* (New York: Harper, 1965).
14. M to Samuel Adams, January 29, 1775 (signed "Marcus Brutus"), M Papers, NYHS.
15. Mason, *The Road to Independence, the Revolutionary Movement in New York, 1773-1777*.
16. *Rivington's Gazetteer*, November 24, 1774.
17. Abbott, *New York in the American Revolution*, p. 130.
18. Morison, *The Oxford History of the American People*, p. 79.
19. Miller, *Origins of the American Revolution*, p. 146.
20. Abbott, *New York in the American Revolution*, p. 138.
21. Ibid., p. 141.

Chapter Six

1. Abbott, *New York in the American Revolution*, p. 143.
2. Bruce Bliven, Jr., *Under the Guns, New York: 1775-1776* (New York: Harper, 1972), p. 2.
3. Abbott, *New York in the American Revolution*, p. 163.

4. Ibid., p. 165.
5. Bliven, *Under the Guns, New York: 1775-1776*, p. 66.
6. Statement by General Lewis Morris, May, 1784, Oswego Historical Society, Oswego, N. Y.
7. M to William Cooper, February 9, 1775, M Papers, NYHS.
8. M to Josiah Quincy, Jr., April 6, 1775, M Papers, NYHS.
9. Bliven, *Under the Guns, New York: 1775-1776*, p. 20.
10. Ibid., p. 36.
11. M to John Jay, October 30, 1775, *Naval Documents of the American Revolution*, Vol. II, p. 645.
12. M to Major General Philip Schuyler, August 9, 1775, M Papers, NYHS.
13. M to John Jay, October 30, 1775, *Naval Documents of the American Revolution*, Vol. II, p. 645.
14. William Goforth to M, 1775, M Papers, NYHS. M to John Jay, October 30, 1775, *Naval Documents of the American Revolution*, Vol. II, p. 645.
15. Colonel Rudolphus Ritzema to M, November 19, 1775, M Papers, NYHS.
16. George Measam to M, March 31, 1776, M Papers, NYHS.
17. Colonel William Goforth to M, November 22, 1775, M Papers, NYHS.
18. M to John Jay, December 24, 1775, *Naval Documents of the American Revolution*, Vol. III, p. 225.
19. Colonel William Goforth to M, March 24, 1776, M Papers, NYHS.
20. Kenneth Roberts, *March to Quebec*, (New York: Doubleday, 1938), p. 284.
21. M to John Jay, in Henry P. Johnston, *The Correspondence and Public Papers of John Jay*, Burt Franklin, ed. (New York: G. P. Putnam's Sons, 1890-93), p. 96.

Chapter Seven

1. Bliven, *Under the Guns, New York: 1775-1776*, p. 24.
2. Staff letter from General Washington to M, March 14, 1776, M Papers, NYHS.
3. M to General Philip Schuyler, March 3, 1776, M Papers, NYHS.
4. M to General Schuyler, March 21, 1776, M Papers, NYHS.
5. General Charles Lee to M, October 26, 1775, *Naval Documents of the American Reolution*, Vol. II, p. 607.

6. General Lee to M, January 28, 1776, Hawkes Collection, Union College.

7. M to John Jay, November 26, 1775, *Naval Documents of the American Revolution,* Vol. II, p. 1146.

8. M to General Schuyler, January 20, 1776, M Papers, NYHS.

9. John Jay to M, December 22, 1775, M Papers, NYHS.

10. Minutes of the New York Committee of Safety, January 22, 1776, *Naval Documents of the American Revolution,* Vol. III, p. 921.

11. John Jay to M, March 21, 1776, M Papers, NYHS.

12. John Jay to M, March 23, 1776, M Papers, NYHS.

13. M to General Schuyler, March 14, 1776, M Papers, NYHS.

14. John Jay to M, March 23, 1776, M Papers, NYHS.

15. Bliven, *Under the Guns, New York: 1775-1776,* p. 123.

16. Ibid., p. 127.

17. Ibid., p. 170.

18. John Graham to M, January 23, 1776, *Naval Documents of the American Revolution,* Vol. III, p. 943.

19. Bliven, *Under the Guns, New York: 1775-1776,* p. 194.

20. William Jay, *The Life of John Jay* (New York: Harper, 1833), Miscellaneous Correspondence, p. 3.

21. John C. Miller, *Triumph of Freedom: 1775/1783* (Boston: Atlantic-Little, Brown, 1948), p. 120.

22. Christopher Ward, *The War of the Revolution,* (New York: Macmillan, 1952), p. 231.

23. John Brick, *They Fought for New York,* (New York: G. P. Putnam's Sons, 1965), p. 47.

24. Ward, *The War of the Revolution,* p. 235.

Chapter Eight

1. Last will and testament of Alexander McDougall, September, 1776, Hawkes Collection, Union College.

2. M Papers, April, 1782, NYHS.

3. Ward, *The War of the Revolution,* p. 262.

4. The Charles Lee Papers, NYHS, 1871-1874.

5. George Washington to M, December 21, 1776, Hawkes Collection, Union College.

6. George Washington to M, December 28, 1776, Hawkes Collection, Union College.

7. George Washington to M, April 12, 1777, Hawkes Collection, Union College.
8. M to George Washington, March 7, 1777, Henry E. Huntington Library, San Marino, Cal.
9. M to George Washington, May 19, 1777, Huntington Library, San Marino, Cal.
10. M to the Committee for the Town of Stamford, December 30, 1776, NYHS.
11. M to State Legislature, April 14, 1777, M Papers, NYHS.
12. M to George Washington, April 17, 1777, Huntington Library, San Marino, Cal.
13. M to General Sir Robert Pigot, April 3, 1777, M Papers, NYHS.
14. General Pigot to M, April 4, 1777, M Papers, NYHS.
15. M to George Washington, March 29, 1777, Huntington Library, San Marino, Cal.
16. George Washington to M, May 1, 1777, Rosenbach Foundation, Philadelphia.
17. Copy of Colonel Livingston's defense, 1777, M Papers, NYHS.
18. "Historical Register of Officers of the Continental Army," Francis B. Heitman, Washington, D.C., 1914.
19. Note from Colonel Henry B. Livingston to M, undated, M Papers, NYHS.
20. "To the Publick," undated, attributed to Colonel Henry B. Livingston, M Papers, NYHS.
21. Ibid.
22. M to Colonel Livingston, undated, M Papers, NYHS.
23. M to George Clinton, June 18, 1777, "Public Papers of George Clinton," State of New York, Vol. II, p. 38.
24. George Washington to M, September 19, 1777, Rosenbach Foundation, Philadelphia.
25. George Washington to M, May 1, 1777, Rosenbach Foundation, Philadelphia.
26. Miller, *Triumph of Freedom: 1775/1783*, p. 176.
27. General Israel Putnam to M, September 15, 1777, M Papers, NYHS.
28. George Washington to M, September 22, 1777, Hawkes Collection, Union College.
29. George Washington to M, September 24, 1777, Hawkes Collection, Union College.
30. Ward, *The War of the Revolution*, p. 362.
31. George Washington's Plan of Attack, October 3, 1777, M Papers, NYHS.
32. Ward, *The War of the Revolution*, p. 368.

33. William Goforth to M, February 20, 1779, M Papers, NYHS.
34. *Journal* (anonymous), October 3, 1777, M Papers, NYHS.
35. John F. Reed, *Campaign to Valley Forge* (Philadelphia: University of Pennsylvania Press, 1965) p. 266.
36. General Nathanael Greene to M, January 25, 1778, M Papers, NYHS.
37. M to General Greene, February 14, 1778, M Papers, NYHS.
38. Griswold, *Washington and the Generals of the American Revolution*, p. 295.

Chapter Nine

1. John McDougall to M, January 7, 1778, Hawkes Collection, Union College.
2. M to George Washington, February 17, 1778, M Papers, NYHS.
3. Ward, *The War of the Revolution*, p. 560.
4. Marquis de Lafayette to M, January 5, 1778, M Papers, NYHS.
5. M to Lafayette, February 18, 1778, M Papers, NYHS.
6. General Greene to M, January 25, 1778, M Papers, NYHS.
7. M to General Greene, February 14, 1778, M Papers, NYHS.
8. General James Varnum to M, February 7, 1778, M Papers, NYHS.
9. General Greene to M, April 16, 1778, M Papers, NYHS.
10. George Washington to M, March 16, 1778, "Public Papers of George Clinton," State of New York, p. 869.
11. M to George Washington, April 13, 1778, Huntington Library, San Marino, Cal.
12. M. Cox, *The Sterling Furnace and the West Point Chain*, private printing, New York, 1906, p. 2.
13. George Washington to M, March 16, 1778, "Public Papers of George Clinton," State of New York, p. 869.
14. M to George Washington, March 29, 1778, Huntington Library, San Marino, Cal.
15. Report, April 18, 1778, M Papers, NYHS.
16. Letter from General James Clinton, April 27, 1778, M Papers, NYHS.
17. George Washington to M, March 25, 1779, Rosenbach Foundation, Philadelphia.
18. George Washington to M, March 28, 1779, Rosenbach Foundation, Philadelphia.
19. Confession of William Cole, March 2, 1779, M Papers, NYHS.

Notes 175

20. Lewis Kennedy to M, April 6, 1779, M Papers, NYHS.
21. "To the Supporters and Defenders of American Freedom," May 20, 1778, Library of Congress.
22. General Greene to M, February 11, 1779, M papers, NYHS.
23. M to General Greene, March 24, 1779, M Papers, NYHS.
24. M to George Clinton, November 5, 1778, "Public Papers of George Clinton," State of New York, p. 244.
25. In December 1788: M to George Washington, December 10, 1778, M Papers, NYHS.
26. M to George Washington, January 11, 1779, Huntington Library, San Marino, Cal.
27. George Washington to M, February 9, 1779, Rosenbach Foundation, Philadelphia.
28. Major Richard Platt to David Tuttle, January 1779, M Papers, NYHS.
29. M to George Washington, June 4, 1779, M Papers, NYHS.
30. M to George Washington, November 11, 1779, M Papers, NYHS.
31. M to George Washington, March 16, 1780, M Papers, NYHS.

Chapter Ten

1. Pierre Van Cortlandt for the Senate of New York, October 6, 1780, Hawkes Collection, Union College.
2. George Washington to M, October 24, 1780, Rosenbach Foundation, Philadelphia.
3. M to George Washington, October 20, 1780, M Papers, NYHS.
4. General Greene to M, October 30, 1780, M Papers, NYHS.
5. General Officers' Memorial to Congress, July 11, 1780, M Papers, NYHS.
6. M to General Greene, August 8, 1780, M Papers, NYHS.
7. M to General Greene, August 15, 1780, M Papers, NYHS.
8. Act of Congress, August 12, 1780, M Papers, NYHS.
9. Lieutenant Colonel John Jameson to George Washington, September 23, 1780, Hawkes Collection, Union College.
10. M to George Washington, November 20, 1783, M Papers, NYHS.
11. George Washington to M, March 31, 1781, Hawkes Collection, Union College.
12. M to George Washington, July 24, 1780, M Papers, NYHS.
13. Charles O. Paullin, *Navy of the American Revolution,* (Chicago: University of Chicago Press, 1906), p. 217.

14. M's declaration to Congress, February 27, 1781, M Papers, NYHS.
15. Draft of questions to Captain John Paul Jones, February 20, 1781, M Papers, NYHS.
16. Samuel E. Morison, *John Paul Jones: A Sailor's Biography* (Boston: Atlantic-Little, Brown, 1959), p. 311.
17. Act of Congress, March 30, 1781, M Papers, NYHS.
18. Major Richard Platt to M, April 15, 1781, M Papers, NYHS.

Chapter Eleven

1. General Greene to M, May 17, 1781, M Papers, NYHS.
2. Major Richard Platt to M, October 18, 1781, M Papers, NYHS.
3. M to George Washington, January 2, 1781, Huntington Library, San Marino, Cal.
4. M to John Lawrance, April 2, 1781, M Papers, NYHS.
5. M to George Clinton, January 27, 1780, and February 8, 1780, M Papers, NYHS.
6. M to General William Heath, November 29, 1781, The Heath Papers, Collection of the Massachusetts Historical Society, p. 315.
7. General Heath to M, December 19, 1781, Heath Papers, Massachusetts Historical Society, p. 328.
8. Testimony of John Lawrance, 1782, M Papers, NYHS.
9. Captain Sumner's report, January 22, 1782, M Papers, NYHS.
10. Colonel Putnam's narrative: January 16, 1782, M Papers, NYHS.
11. Nathan Goodale to M, January 23, 1782, M Papers, NYHS.
12. General Heath to M, January 18, 1782, M Papers, NYHS.
13. M to George Washington, January 27, 1782, M Papers, NYHS.
14. George Washington to M, February 3, 1782, Hawkes Collection, Union College.
15. M to George Washington, 1782, M Papers, NYHS.
16. M's summary of his defense, 1782, M Papers, NYHS.
17. The Heath Papers, Massachusetts Historical Society, p. 402.
18. M to George Washington, August 23, 1782, M Papers, NYHS.
19. General Stirling to M, August 30, 1782, M Papers, NYHS.
20. M to General Stirling, November 12, 1782, M Papers, NYHS.
21. General Stirling to M, December 4, 1782, M Papers, NYHS.
22. M to Stirling, December 14, 1782, M Papers, NYHS.
23. James Duane to M, August 28, 1782, M Papers, NYHS.

Chapter Twelve

1. M to George Clinton, March 28, 1782, M Papers, NYHS.
2. M to George Washington, August 26, 1782, M Papers, NYHS.
3. M to Washington, November 6, 1782, M Papers, NYHS.
4. Officers to Washington, 1782, M Papers, NYHS.
5. Richard H. Kahn, "The Inside History of the Newburgh Conspiracy: America and the Coup d'Etat," *William and Mary Quarterly*, Third series, Vol. XXVII, No. 2 (April 1970), provides insight into the army's restiveness.
6. M to unknown, December 12, 1782, Huntington Library, San Marino, Cal.
7. Edmund Cody Burnett, *The Continental Congress* (New York: Norton, 1941), p. 553.
8. Ibid.
9. Ibid.
10. Russell F. Weigley, *History of the United States Army* (New York: Macmillan, 1967), p. 76.
11. M to General Henry Knox, February 8, 1783, M Papers, NYHS.
12. General Knox to M, February 21, 1783, M Papers, NYHS.
13. General Knox to M, March 12, 1783, M Papers, NYHS.
14. Miller, *Triumph of Freedom: 1775/1783*, p. 673.
15. George Washington to "Gentlemen," March 15, 1783, M Papers, NYHS.
16. Ibid.
17. Resolution of the Army, March 15, 1783, M Papers, NYHS.
18. Weigley, *History of the United States Army*, p. 77.
19. Abbott, *New York in the American Revolution*, p. 268.
20. M to George Washington, October 5, 1783, M Papers, NYHS.
21. M to Chief Justice Richard Morris, December 25, 1783, and Morris to M, December 28, 1783, M Papers, NYHS.
22. Colonel Tallmadge, quoted by Sons of the Revolution of the State of New York, Pamphlet, New York.
23. Henry W. Domett, *A History of the Bank of New York, 1784-1884*, (1884; reprinted, New York: Greenwood Press, 1969), pp. 6-7.
24. M to Alexander Stewart, 1785, M Papers, NYHS.
25. M to William McDougall, September 11, 1785, M Papers, NYHS.
26. *New York Gazetteer*, June 13, 1786.
27. Ibid.

Bibliography

*T*his bibliography is confined to primary sources and the most important secondary sources used by the author. An excellent detailed bibliography of the American Revolutionary period appears in *The War of American Independence* by Don Higginbotham, published in 1971 by Macmillan. Excellent sources for the Revolutionary period in New York are provided by Bernard Mason in *The Road to Independence, the Revolutionary Movement in New York, 1773-1777*, (Lexington: University of Kentucky Press, 1966).

Books

Abbott, Wilbur C. *New York in the American Revolution.* New York, 1929.
Bliven, Bruce, Jr. *Under the Guns. New York: 1775-1776.* New York, 1972.
Brick, John. *They Fought for New York.* New York, 1965.
Bridenbaugh, Carl. *Cities in Revolt.* New York, 1955.
Burnett, Edmund C. *The Continental Congress.* New York, 1941.
Clark, William B., ed. *Naval Documents of the American Revolution.* 6 vols. Washington, D.C., 1964.
Colden, Cadwallader. *The Letters and Papers of Cadwallader Colden, 1711-1775,* 9 vols. (New York Historical Society, *Collections*) New York, 1918-1937.

Cox, M. *The Sterling Furnace and the West Point Chain.* New York, 1906.
Domett, Henry W. *A History of the Bank of New York, 1784-1884.* New York, 1969.
Fish, Stuyvesant. *The New York Privateers, 1756-1763.* New York, 1945.
Griswold, W. W. *Washington and the Generals of the Revolution.* Philadelphia, 1866.
Heath, William. *The Heath Papers.* Massachusetts Historical Society, Parts I-III, *Collections).* Boston, 1878-1905.
Heitman, Francis B. *Historical Register of Officers of the Continental Army.* Washington, 1914.
Jay, John. *The Correspondence and Public Papers of John Jay.* Henry P. Johnston, ed. New York, 1890.
Jay, William. *The Life of John Jay.* New York, 1833.
Jensen, Merrill. *The Founding of a Nation: A History of the American Revolution, 1763-1776.* New York, 1968.
Jones, Thomas. *History of New York During the Revolutionary War.* Edward F. DeLancey, ed., 2 vols. New York, 1879.
Lee, Charles. *The Lee Papers . . . 1754-1811,* 4 vols., (New-York Historical Society, *Collections)* IV-VII. New York, 1872-1875.
Lyman, Susan. *The Story of New York.* New York, 1964.
MacLean, J. P. *An Historical Account of the Settlements of Scotch Highlanders in America Prior to the Peace of 1783.* Baltimore, 1968.
Maier, Pauline. *From Resistance to Revolution.* New York, 1974.
Miller, John C. *Origins of the American Revolution.* Boston, 1943.
———. *Triumph of Freedom: 1775/1783.* Boston, 1948.
Mitchell, Broadus. *Alexander Hamilton: Youth to Maturity.* New York, 1957.
Moncreiffe of That Ilk and Hicks, David. *The Highland Clans.* London, 1967.
Morison, Samuel Eliot. *John Paul Jones: A Sailor's Biography.* Boston, 1959.
Morris, Richard B. *Encyclopedia of American History.* New York, 1965.
Paullin, Charles O. *Navy of the American Revolution.* Chicago, 1906.
Phelps, I. N. *The Iconography of Manhattan Island,* 6 vols. New York, 1915-1928.
Princeton University. *General Catalogue of Princeton University, 1746-1906.* Princeton, 1908.
Reed, John F. *Campaign to Valley Forge.* Philadelphia, 1965.
Roberts, Kenneth. *March to Quebec.* New York, 1938.
Stokes, Anson Phelps and Pfeffer, Leo. *Church and State in the United States.* New York, 1964.
Ward, Christopher. *The War of the Revolution,* 2 vols., New York, 1951.

Washington, George. *Writings of Washington*, John C. Fitzpatrick, ed., 39 vols. Washington, D.C., 1931-1944.
Weigley, Russell F. *History of the United States Army*. New York, 1967.
 and Soldier, 1732-1786, Ph. D. dissertation, Fordham University, New
Williamson, Audrey. *Wilkes: A Friend to Liberty*. New York, 1974.

Periodicals

Boston Gazette, February 26, 1770.
New England Quarterly, Vol. XXXII, No. 1, March 1964.
New York Gazette, April 9, 1770, October 3, 1757.
New York Gazetteer, June 13, 1786.
The New-York Historical Society Quarterly, Vol. XLIX, No. 4, October 1965.
New York History, Vol. XXXII, No. 1, January 1951.
New York Journal, March 29, 1770; April 19, 1770; May 3, 1770; June 7, 1770.
New York Mercury, October 17, 1757; November 7, 1757; February 20, 1758; May 15, 1758.
Pennsylvania Journal, March 22, 1770.
Rivington's Gazetteer, November 24, 1774.
William and Mary Quarterly, Third series, Vol. XXVII, No. 1, January 1970; Vol. XXII, No. 2, April 1965; Vol. XXVII, No. 2, April 1970.

Manuscripts

Baptismal Register, 1732, 1735, 1737, Kildalton Parish, Isle of Islay, Scotland.
Boston Committee of Correspondence Manuscripts, New York Public Library.
W. Wright Hawkes Collection, Union College, Schenectady, N. Y.
Alexander McDougall Papers, New-York Historical Society, New York.
McDougall, Alexander, Manuscripts, Henry E. Huntington Library, San Marino, Cal.
McDougall, Alexander, Manuscripts, Rosenbach Foundation, Philadelphia.
Memoirs and a Journal of the Presbyterian Congregation in the City of New York, The First Presbyterian Church, New York.
Morris, Lewis, statement, Oswego County Historical Society, Oswego, N.Y.
Ramsay, Mrs. Iain, Family Records, Isle of Islay, Scotland.
Shannon, Sister Anna Madeleine, *General Alexander McDougall, Citizen and Soldier, 1732-1786*, Ph. D. dissertation, Fordham University, New York, 1957.

Index

Adams, John, xi, 51-53, 57, 59, 62
Adams, Samuel, 45, 47, 49, 50, 53, 57, 58, 59, 137
Alexander, William (Lord Stirling), 79, 144, 145, 146
Allen, Ethan, 69
Alsop, John, 53, 55, 79
Andre, John, 133
Argyle Patent, 4, 5, 9, 156
Arnold, Benedict, 69, 71, 72, 90, 128, 132, 133
Asia, 66, 67, 78

Barré, Isaac, 22, 23
Bogert, Cornelius, 95
Boston Committee of Correspondence, 44, 47, 48
Boston Massacre, 28, 39, 40
Boston Port Bill, 45, 49
Boston Tea Party, 43, 44, 45
Bostwick, David, 20
Botta, Alexander, 85
Brooks, John, 148, 150

Bunker Hill, Battle of, 62, 82
Burgoyne, John, 107, 114, 123

Campbell, Lachlan, 3, 4, 5, 8, 26
Carleton, Guy, 72, 90, 101, 148
Carr, John, 35
Chapman, Abner, 118, 119
Charleston, S. C., 24, 80, 81
Church of England, 52, 156
Cincinnati, Society of the, 153
Clarke, George, 3, 4, 5
Clinton, George, 25, 36, 100, 118, 122, 123, 142, 144, 147, 155
Clinton, Henry, 80, 127, 139, 140
Colden, Cadwallader, 5, 26, 30
Congress, 46, 48, 49, 50, 51-53, 56, 59, 65, 68, 69, 87, 91, 115, 119, 121, 122, 124, 125, 129-137, 148, 149, 152
Conway, Thomas, 111-115
Cornwallis, Lord, 139, 140, 141

De Lancey, James, 27, 54, 75
De Lancey, Oliver, 45
De Lancey Family, 16, 18, 23, 25,

26, 29, 33-35, 46, 47, 52, 55, 62
Dickinson, John, 49, 50, 54
Duane, James, 48, 52, 53, 55, 146
Dudington, William, 43
Du Simitière, Pierre, 31, 32

Emmerich, Colonel, 120, 121

First New York Regiment, 66, 89
First Presbyterian Church, New York City, xiii, 9, 20, 157
Fisher, Elijah, 154
Fort George, N. Y., 18, 22, 51, 66, 67, 155
Fort Lee, N. J., 90
Fort St. Johns, Quebec, 69, 70, 71
Fort Washington, N. Y., 90, 95
Franklin, Benjamin, xii, 37, 38
Fraunces' Tavern, 18, 24, 46, 62, 155

Gaspee, 43
Gates, Horatio, 111, 112, 114, 115, 123
General Barrington, 14
Germantown, Battle of, 102-105, 111, 114
Glover's and Hutchinson's Regiments, 84
Goforth, William, 68, 69, 72
Golden Hill, Battle of, 28
Graham, John, 80
Greene, Nathanael, 76, 87, 103-106, 113-115, 118, 122, 129-131, 139, 140, 147, 155

Hamilton, Alexander, xii, 55, 67, 89, 135, 150, 155, 156
Hampden Hall, 34
Hancock, John, 58, 59
Haslet, John, 90
Hastings, Hugh, 28
Heath, William, 88, 141-145
Henry, Patrick, 57
Hessians, 88-91, 120
Hickey, Thomas, 81

Hicks, Whitehead, 25, 28
Horsmanden, Daniel, 29
Howe, William, 76, 80, 82, 90, 91, 92, 95, 101-103, 105, 106, 111

Islay, Isle of, Scotland, 4, 6, 8

Jameson, John, 133
Jay, John, 59, 64, 67-69, 72, 73, 77, 78, 81, 133
Jefferson, Thomas, xi
Jones, John Paul, 135-136
Jones, Thomas, xii, 15

Keffler, Francis, 13
Kennedy, Lewis, 120, 121
King George's War, 11
King's College, 17, 55, 75
Knox, Henry, 104, 118, 150-153, 155
Kosciusko, Thaddeus, 116, 155

Lafayette, Marquis de, xi, 112, 113
Lamb, John, 27, 44, 63
Lawrance, John, 124, 133, 142
Lee, Charles, 65, 76, 77, 79, 81, 90
Lexington, Battle of, 58
Liberty Pole, 24, 27, 31, 32, 34, 42, 55, 58
Lispenard, Leonard, 55
Livingston, Henry B., 97-100
Livingston, Philip, 53, 79
Livingston family, 15, 16, 23, 25, 52
Long Island, Battle of, 82-83
Louisbourg, Battle of, 11
Low, Isaac, 48, 52, 53

McDougall, Alexander, 4; youth, 6, 8; sailor, 11-15; merchant, 16; description, 19, 21, 25, 26, 28, 29; jail, 30, 32, 34, 35; trial, 36, 41, 43, 46, 47, 49-53, 55, 56, 58, 59, 64, 65-69, 75, 78-81, 83; Long Island, 84, 85, 87, 91, 94, 96, 97-99, 101; Germantown, 102-105, 106, 107, 113, 114, 116, 119,

120-128; Congress, 129-137; court martial, 142-146, 147, 148, 150-157
McDougall, Ann (Nancy), 11, 20
McDougall, Eleanor, 4, 156
McDougall, Elizabeth (daughter), 11, 20, 52, 87
McDougall, Elizabeth (sister), 4
McDougall, Hannah, 21, 52, 87, 92, 123, 124, 141, 148
McDougall, John (brother), 4
McDougall, John (nephew), 109, 110
McDougall, John Alexander, 11, 20, 69, 71
McDougall, Mary, 4, 20
McDougall, Ranald (father), 4, 6, 8, 9, 10
McDougall, Ranald Stephen (son), 11, 20, 69, 72, 73, 87, 92
McDougall, Stephen, 11, 14, 19-21
McDougall, William, 19
Mabee, Simon, 94
Madison, James, 150
Mifflin, Thomas, 84, 88, 112, 114, 115
Montayne's Tavern, 27, 33
Montgomery, Richard, 69, 71, 72
Montreal, 70-72
Morgan, Daniel, 72, 140
Morris, Gouverneur, 47, 48, 59
Morris, Lewis, 64
Morristown, N. J., 91, 106, 110
Muhlenberg, Peter, 104
Mutiny Act, 24

Newport, R. I., 43
New York Assembly, 5, 6, 24, 26, 27, 34, 36, 37
New York Committee of Correspondence, 46, 56
New York Committee of Fifty-One, 46, 48, 52-55
New York Committee of One Hundred, 59

New York Committee of Safety, 59, 78, 79
New York Committee of Sixty, 58, 59
New York *Gazette*, 32
New York *Gazetteer*, 157
New York Legislature, 129, 130
New York Provincial Congress, 59, 62, 81
New York Tea Party, 45
North, Lord, 43, 50, 53

Ogden, Matthias, 148, 150

Paine, Thomas, 62
Parliament, 38, 42, 44, 45, 48, 59
Parker, James, 25, 29, 35, 36
Paterson, John, 143
Peekskill, N. Y., 94-96, 98, 107, 116, 118, 124, 126, 127
Pemberton, Reverend, 9, 10
Philadelphia Committee of Forty-Three, 54
Platt, Richard, 97, 126, 137, 141
Presbyterian Church, 16, 18, 52, 56
Putnam, Israel, 102

Quebec, 72
Quincy, Josiah, 65

Revere, Paul, 44, 45, 47, 49, 58
Ritzema, Rudolphus, 68, 71, 72
Rivington, James, 63, 64
Rush, Benjamin, 111

Saratoga, Battle of, 107, 114
Schuyler, Philip, 65, 66, 68, 69, 76, 77, 100
Scott, Charles, 104, 105
Scott, John Morin, 23, 52, 79
Sears, Isaac, 23, 28, 35, 41, 44, 46, 47, 50, 54, 59, 63
Sons of Liberty, 23-29, 33-36, 40, 42-46, 54, 56, 58, 63, 96, 121
Sparks, Jared, xiii

Stamp Act, 21, 24
Stephen, Adam, 104-106
Steuben, Friedrich von, 153, 155
Stewart, Alexander, 20, 21
Suffolk Resolves, 57
Sullivan, John, 104, 105

Tea Act, 43, 44
Thomson, Charles, 49, 50
Ticonderoga, 69, 101
Tories, 27, 33, 34, 36, 56, 68, 77, 79, 81, 94, 121, 153, 154
Trenton, Battle of, 91, 92
Trevelyan, George Macauley, 85
Tryon, William, 44, 51, 61, 67, 76, 77, 80
Tyger, 12, 13

Valley Forge, 111-115
Varnum, James, 115

Washington, George, xi, 61, 62, 65, 68, 75, 76, 81-84, 87, 88, 90-92, 97, 98, 100, 102-105, 107, 111, 114-116, 118-120, 124, 125, 130, 134, 140, 143, 144, 151, 152, 154, 155
Wayne, Anthony, 104
Westchester County, N. Y., 94
West Point, N. Y., 116, 127, 142, 148
Whigs, 35, 42, 58, 68
White Plains, Battle of, 88
Wilkes, John, xii, 30, 34
Willett, Marinus, 96

Zenger, John Peter, 33

About the Author

William L. MacDougall, former Washington correspondent for the *Los Angeles Times*, is senior editor for *U.S. News & World Report*. He covered Bicentennial and cultural affairs for that magazine.

Recent Titles in
CONTRIBUTIONS IN AMERICAN HISTORY
Series Editor: *Jon L. Wakelyn*

Confederate Women
Bell Irvin Wiley

Battles Lost and Won: Essays from Civil War History
John T. Hubbell, Editor

Beyond the Civil War Synthesis: Political Essays of the Civil War Era
Robert P. Swierenga, Editor

Roosevelt and Romanism: Catholics and American Diplomacy, 1937-1945
George Q. Flynn

Roots of Tragedy: The United States and the Struggle for Asia, 1945-1953
Lisle A. Rose

Henry A. Wallace and American Foreign Policy
J. Samuel Walker

Retreat from Reform: The Prohibition Movement in the United States, 1890-1913
Jack S. Blocker, Jr.

A New Birth of Freedom: The Republican Party and Freedmen's Rights, 1861 to 1866
Herman Belz

When Farmers Voted Red: The Gospel of Socialism in the Oklahoma Countryside, 1910-1924
Garin Burbank

Essays in Nineteenth-Century American Legal History
Wythe Holt, Editor

Henry Highland Garnet: A Voice of Black Radicalism in the Nineteenth Century
Joel Schor

The Prophet's Army: Trotskyists in America, 1928-1941
Constance Ashton Myers

Working Dress in Colonial and Revolutionary America
Peter F. Copeland